BO STORIES

Co-Authors/Bo Stories

JACK ETKIN
BOB NIGHTENGALE
KEVIN SCARBINSKY
RICK WEINBERG

Co-Editors/Bo Stories

JOE HOPPEL
STEVE ZESCH

Illustrated by

Bill Wilson

The Sporting News

Published in the United States by THE SPORTING NEWS Publishing Co., 1212 North Lindbergh Boulevard, St. Louis, Missouri 63132.

ISBN: 0-89204-350-4
10 9 8 7 6 5 4 3 2 1

First Edition

Table
of
Contents

Introduction

When he steps into the batting cage, all activity stops and eyes are glued on the mighty swing that launches baseballs into uncharted territory. When he steps into the batter's box during a game, electricity and a sense of anticipation fill the air. Football fans buzz with excitement every time he takes a handoff, waiting for that incredible burst of speed that can literally launch him toward the end zone.

Meet Bo Jackson, the new-generation, high-tech athlete; the man for all seasons who makes his living playing two professional sports—and playing them at a level unknown to many of his peers.

Beyond the incredible athletic talents packed into his powerful frame, Bo brings to the national sports scene an almost mystical quality that promotes expectations of super-human feats and unusual athletic prowess.

Prodigious home runs, 90-yard touchdown runs and howitzer-type throws from the outfield are but a few of the regular occurrences that feed the growing legend of this former Heisman Trophy winner while vaulting him into the select circle of one-name superstars.

Bo Stories chronicles some of those feats while providing a glimpse of Bo through the eyes of past and present coaches, teammates, opponents and scouts. This book is not meant to glorify Bo Jackson beyond his present accomplishments. It is, rather, an attempt to put those accomplishments into perspective while taking a fun look at one of the most exciting and amazing athletes in sports history—regardless of what he does in the 1990s.

Odds are that Bo will do plenty. But even if he doesn't, there is little doubt that years from now fathers and grandfathers will be telling *Bo Stories* of their own.

THE EARLY YEARS

Bo Jackson probably doesn't qualify as the quintessential problem child. He managed to stay in school and stay out of jail, which was some trick for a kid who stole bikes, once clubbed his cousin (a girl) with a baseball bat and, for a prank, broke into a neighbor's hog pen with his friends to stone to death a hog or two.

"I was the one caught because everybody knew the 'bad little Jackson kid,' " Bo said of the slaughter. "But the man who owned the hogs was a minister and said that if I was grounded for the summer and did all his chores around the house, he wouldn't press charges."

OK, so Bo ran a little wild in the streets growing up in Bessemer, Ala. He was one of 10 children raised by his mother in a three-room house on the outskirts of Birmingham. He had only occasional contact with his father, who lived across town, and his older brothers always seemed to be away, too. With no older male around to talk to, Bo ran loose.

Jackson admits that he was the bully in school. He stole lunch money from sixth-graders when he was in the third grade, he fought regularly and found mischief at every street corner.

"I wasn't bigger than the other kids," he said, "but they thought I was tough because I used to take off my shirt and let my big brother hit me in the stomach. If somebody got me mad, I'd just hit them with a rock upside the head. I threw rocks all the time.

"My older brother and cousins said I was tough like a wild boar. After awhile, they just cut it short and called me 'Bo.' "

Bo's mother cut plenty of switches from the cherry tree, but the lessons usually wore off about the same time the sting from the whippings did. Jackson said he didn't change his ways until he was 16. Many of his friends never did.

"Now, whenever I go home," he said, "my hometown depresses the hell out of me. It's simply because when I go back there, I see the people I grew up with and see they aren't doing anything. It's pitiful. That's why when I go home, I just visit my mom and aunt and nieces and nephews, and then I'm back out of there."

Bo tried drugs once in his life. Some of the old crowd made drugs a way of life.

"I tried them once," Bo remembered. "I was in the ninth grade, I was coming out of a social studies class and I found a brown bag in the hall. There were three marijuana joints inside. I smoked one. After that experience, I said I'd never do drugs again. And I haven't and never will.

"It's all right to go out and party, but when you go out and do drugs, you don't know what to expect. You're asking for it. It's like (former Maryland basketball star) Len Bias. I feel sorry for the fact that his life had to end at such a young age, but I don't fault anyone but Len Bias for doing what he did."

Bo admits he lost "a whole lot of friends" because of his hard-line opinion of drug users. As far as Jackson is concerned, anyone who takes a hit or two can hit the high road.

"There were friends who did drugs, but I cut myself off from them," he said. "I didn't know they did drugs until the time they did it in front of me. I said, 'No, I've grown up. I've become an adult now, and I know what's wrong and what's right. And the stuff that you're doing is absolutely wrong and I want no part of it.'"

□

When Bo Jackson was in high school, his mother couldn't bring herself to watch her son compete in the sport she never wanted him to play. Bo was bigger, stronger and tougher than most mature men, but Florence Bond feared for the safety of her child on the football field.

"When I look back now, it's kind of funny," Jackson said. "My mom never wanted me to play football, but she never told me that. She just said, 'Whatever you want to do, I'm backing you 100 percent.'"

Bo said his mother supported him in absentia, never once making the trip to McAdory High on game day. Jackson remembers her locking him out of the house when he returned home from his first few practices. When he started making headlines on the local sports page, however, mom began to soften.

But even then, if Florence Bond had to pick a field of dreams for her son, she probably would have chosen a baseball diamond.

"I dragged her to a couple of baseball games," Bo said, "and the first game she went to, I hit the longest home run in high school history when the Yankees were watching. I hit it to straightaway center field, about 500, 550 feet.

"When she saw that baseball wasn't a rough sport, I think she liked that best. But then when I got to Auburn, I couldn't keep her away from the football stadium. She was trying to tell the referees what to do and everything. She became a regular Howard Cosell."

□

"You think he's quiet now? Well, he's an extrovert compared to the way he grew up," recalled Dick Atchison, Jackson's football coach at McAdory High in McCalla, Ala.

Quiet, private, independent—they all applied to the schoolboy with the extraordinary athletic talent.

Bo had a speech impediment, a stutter, that made him terrified to read aloud in class. For most of his high school years, he essentially left in the morning for school, went to class, practiced whatever sport was in season and returned home.

"Really, he didn't hang around with the other kids," Atchison said. "Bo's senior year, if you walked into the gym, he'd be sitting in the corner by himself, studying. Maybe other kids would be sitting somewhere else, talking and jiving, but not Bo. He had some very close friends, but he wasn't as outgoing as he is now."

The transition to college and the pressures of football were torturous at times for the new kid on campus with the chiseled physique.

"When he was at Auburn his freshman and sophomore years, he used to sit in his room and listen to gospel music," Atchison said. "He used to call me on Saturday nights. Now, they would play a ball game Saturday afternoon. Bo would call collect and he would really be down. I mean, to the point of wanting to come home.

"Bo would say, 'I played ball this afternoon, I came back and sat in my room.'

"I'd say, 'Bo, what do the other players do?' and he told me they went to parties." Atchison tried to encourage Jackson to join them. "He'd say, 'I don't want to. I just don't like that.' And he'd sit in his room.

"I think things got better his junior and senior years. He started dating and doing some things. But boy, his first two years there, he was almost a recluse."

□

Despite what Michael Jordan says in the Nike commercial, Bo doesn't know basketball. Jackson confesses that his hoops genius begins and ends with his ability to throw down monster jams.

"Bo hated basketball," said Terry Brasseale, his baseball coach at McAdory High. Yet Jackson left Brasseale awestruck with one simple move on the hardwood.

Bo was sitting in the gymnasium in his street clothes as basketball practice wound down one afternoon. The team filtered out of the gym and Jackson cased the area to make sure he was alone.

"He looked around, then went over to pick up a ball off the floor," said Brasseale, who had ducked out of sight. "He took a couple of strides, went up and dunked behind his head."

Bo walked back to the bleachers, picked up his schoolbooks and left.

"I guess," Brasseale reasoned, "he just wanted to know that he could do it."

So he just did it.

□

McAdory High slugging sensation Bo Jackson skied a fly ball to short left field. The outfielder, as was usually the case when Jackson dug in, was playing with his back to the fence. As he began the long run in, the tiny speck disappeared in the lights and fell safely to earth.

Third-base coach Terry Brasseale looked toward second base to hold up Jackson—who was already steaming to third.

"I just pointed him to the plate," Brasseale said, "and he scored without a throw."

□

McAdory High football Coach Dick Atchison knew three into two would not go. But he also figured that when Vincent (Bo) Jackson was part of the equation, there was such a thing as a solution.

With three sterling running backs competing for two spots entering the 1981 season, Atchison had no choice but to resaddle one of his thoroughbreds as a plow horse at fullback. And who better than the multi-talented Jackson, who also happened to play defensive end, kick off on the special teams and boot the extra points and field goals.

Bo would reward Atchison with 1,173 rushing yards and 17 touchdowns, but not without suffering through some growing pains.

In the second game of the season, the coach recalled, Bo fumbled four times, none of them caused by contact. The following Monday—on Labor Day, no less—Atchison rode herd on the team through a seven-hour practice. He leaned on Bo particularly hard, assigning him to the scout team and ordering him to run extra laps.

"We tried to get Bo's attention," Atchison said.

They almost got his resignation. Three days later, Jackson was set to leave the team until a long talk with the coach smoothed over relations.

"That Friday night," Atchison said, "he had a tremendous game. We won. From that day on, he was a model guy. He never missed a practice. The guys accepted him back. I just walked in the locker room after the game and said, 'Welcome back, Bo.' "

□

During his prep baseball career, Jackson was close to automatic as a man of steal: In 91 attempts, Bo stole 90 bases.

"The only time he got caught, he stumbled getting away from first base and still nearly beat the throw," McAdory Coach Terry Brasseale said. "If he got to first base, it usually didn't take him long to get to second."

According to his high school coaches, Bo Jackson is a clean freak. Maybe not on the order of Michael Jackson and his hyperbaric chamber, but Bo sometimes felt a compulsion to hit the showers *before* games, football Coach Dick Atchison said.

Baseball Coach Terry Brasseale can tell you a story about the well-scrubbed senior who chose to quit the baseball team rather than muss up his clothes in sliding practice. Really.

Each year, Brasseale staged his sliding drills on a patch of sideline on the McAdory football field, wetting down what little grass there was on the trampled sward. Since the sliding pit turned into a mud bog within minutes, the coach advised his players to turn out for practice in their oldest clothes.

That wasn't the answer for Bo, who sidled up to Brasseale to discuss a one-day leave of absence. "Coach, you know I don't like to get dirty," said the senior who would slug 20 home runs, tying a national prep record, and bat .447.

"OK," Brasseale said, "just make sure you turn your uniform in. We don't need you."

"Fine," Jackson said.

For 24 hours, Brasseale wondered about the wisdom of his stand. When the players assembled for sliding practice the following day, Bo was not among them. In the distance, however, Brasseale heard a voice calling his name. It was coming from a young man dressed in a white shirt, white pants and white shoes. It was Jackson.

"He came running down the hill," Brasseale said, "he got in line and when it was his turn he slid head first."

□

For a kid who walked around with a howitzer hanging from his right shoulder, Jackson hated to pitch in high school. After some figurative arm-twisting, however, he was persuaded to help out a McAdory pitching staff that was particularly lean during his junior season.

Bo finished that year with a 9-1 record, but one game stands out as testament to his insistence on doing or having things his own way.

Jackson met privately with Coach Terry Brasseale (as Bo often did to discuss weighty matters) about this hated business of pitching. The coach instructed him to think of the team and not himself. "Be ready to take your turn in the rotation," Brasseale imparted.

Jackson found himself on the mound as scheduled. During warmups, he threw every pitch at warp speed, straight down the chute. It was the perfect smoke screen for what was about to unfold.

Bo's first pitch of the game arrived high and tight to the leadoff hitter.

Ball one. His second delivery was exactly identical, as were the third and fourth. Ball four.

After each pitch, Bo glanced toward Brasseale, who watched stoically as four straight batters reached base on four pitches each. The fourth base on balls brought the McAdory coach out to the mound. "You are in the game until your arm falls off," he informed Jackson, no matter how many bad pitches he intentionally threw.

The game resumed, and Bo walked the next three batters. Brasseale had seen enough. He yanked Jackson and sent him off for a marathon run as punishment for his insubordination.

"He was going to show me he didn't want to pitch," the coach said. "Eventually, he pitched."

□

Jackson had a fondness for track in high school that transcended his love of baseball and football. By his senior year, Bo had parlayed a deal to choose between track and baseball whenever the two sports had scheduled events for the same day.

"We let him choose," said Dick Atchison, the track and football coach at McAdory High. "He would always go for the bigger game."

That option didn't sit well with the moving pack of baseball scouts that gathered every time and everywhere McAdory played.

On one road date the scouts had designated especially important, their number swelled far past the usual 15 to 20 members. "Which one's Jackson?" one of the newcomers asked Coach Terry Brasseale.

"None of them," Brasseale said, breaking the news that Bo was running in a track meet that day.

When Jackson did travel with the baseball team, he usually rode in the coach's car to escape the scouting posse that chased the bus. During one such trip, it was clear Bo would have rather been elsewhere.

"You reckon I can make money running track after college, without playing baseball or football?" he asked Brasseale. "You think I could make a living just running track?"

The scouting crush nearly overwhelmed player and coach alike during Bo's final year. Brasseale was hounded about playing Jackson in center field instead of his customary spot at shortstop, about letting Bo take extended batting practice at the expense of the other players.

At one point, Brasseale had to enter the hospital for a minor operation, leaving Jackson to fend for himself. Bo showed up at the hospital one afternoon, a visit that stretched past one hour, then another and another.

Brasseale finally pleaded that he was going to have to get some rest.

That was quite all right, said Bo, who nevertheless explained that he wasn't able to leave just yet because the scouts had staked out his own house as well as all of his friends'.

Said Brasseale: "It was misery for him . . . and me that year."

□

The McAdory baseball Yellow Jackets were enjoying an outdoor banquet after Jackson's senior season. The players were romping about in the swimming area at Oak Mountain State Park. Bo was standing by himself, which wasn't particularly unusual for the introspective senior.

"He was in about waist-deep water," Coach Terry Brasseale recalled. "He looks around to see if anybody's watching him. All of a sudden he does a complete back flip and lands on his feet. That's hard enough on land, let alone in water up to your waist."

□

The idea of the all-around athlete has held appeal since the ancient Greeks introduced the five-event pentathlon to Olympic competition in 708 B.C. A couple of hundred years and a century later, the 10-event decathlon provided the perfect showcase for a prep track star named Bo Jackson to exhibit his remarkable athletic prowess in the Alabama state championships.

As much a track legend in Alabama as a football-baseball idol, Jackson had the smoke to establish standing state records in the 100-yard dash (9.59 seconds) and 60-yard high hurdles (7.29 seconds), the agility to set the standard in the triple jump (48 feet, 7¼ inches) and high jump (6 feet, 9 inches), and the muscle to hurl the javelin, discus and shot put for eye-catching distances, despite a crude form. Bo's record leap of 22 feet, 6½ inches in the long jump was only recently eclipsed.

The one thing he lacked was the disciplined endurance of the distance runner. According to McAdory Coach Dick Atchison, "he hated the mile," which just happened to be the final event in the decathlon at the state finals.

As a sophomore, Bo failed to score a point in the mile and finished second in the overall standings. He held up slightly better over the distance the following year, earning just enough points in the event to secure the decathlon title outright.

By his senior year, Bo had grown wiser. He calculated the number of points he'd need to cinch the title through nine events, thus sparing himself the agony of the dreaded mile.

The pole vault presented a challenge in itself, however, mostly because

When Bo Jackson competed in the Alabama state track meet for McAdory High, he used a borrowed pole to clear more than 12 feet in the decathlon.

McAdory High didn't even own a pole. After some fast talking, the coaches borrowed a pole from one of the other schools, most of whom were loathe to watch the 215-pound Jackson test equipment with a test weight of 180 pounds.

Bo met the challenge. He cleared the bar at better than 12 feet, wrapping up his second decathlon championship and, just as satisfying, earning a breather in the mile.

Bo's flair for the dramatic in track had been documented during his junior year. At a 1981 outdoor meet, Jackson was locked in a tight battle in the triple jump through the preliminary round.

In the final round of three jumps, an opponent pushed the barrier past 47 feet, shattering the state record by more than three feet.

"Everybody in the stands is going, 'Oh, that record will never be broken,'" Atchison recalled.

Bo Jackson, however, still had one attempt left. He hopped, skipped and jumped . . . all the way to 48 feet, 7¼ inches, more than a foot farther than the jumper who had just set the "unbreakable" record.

"Had that kid jumped 48 feet," Atchison said, "Bo might have gone 49."

One week in the life of high school senior Bo Jackson:

Monday, Tuesday and Thursday: Bo plays for the McAdory High baseball team in the 40-team Jefferson County tournament.

Friday and Saturday: Bo wins the decathlon at the Alabama state track championship.

Sunday: With McAdory in the final round of the Jefferson County tournament, Bo plays both games of a doubleheader. He pitches the championship game, striking out 15 batters, and McAdory wins the tournament's small-school division.

□

If pride goeth before a fall, Bo Jackson would leave a team before sacrificing his self-respect.

Leather jackets were in vogue at McAdory High in the early 1980s, for students and staff alike. Baseball Coach Terry Brasseale knew a thing or two about fashion and bought a snappy number for himself.

What Brasseale didn't know was that leather coats have a way of changing hands through unlawful means. When he discovered his coat missing one day, he went looking for his star player, Jackson.

Brasseale didn't actually suspect Bo as a thief. He did, however, believe Jackson ran with some people of questionable character, the kind who might take a man's new leather coat. He caught up with Bo in the locker room, explained the situation and asked whether he'd help retrieve the jacket.

Bo walked to his locker, removed the three baseball uniforms he had been issued and handed them to the coach. He was insulted that Brasseale would question his ability to choose friends.

"He said he didn't think he could play for me if I thought that," said Brasseale, who quickly apologized for what he had implied. Bo remained on the team.

□

Bo Jackson, all-state senior fullback, blocked for McAdory High's two senior halfbacks more than he carried the ball himself. Bo had a formidable frame, meaning opponents suffered the worst of it physically when he crashed the line ahead of the ballcarrier.

Coach Dick Atchison swears that on one play against Leeds at Birmingham's Legion Field, Bo "dominoed down five guys" and the halfback followed the hole for 65 yards and a touchdown.

Jackson enjoyed body contact on defense, too. Lined up at defensive end, he had the strength to sweep aside linemen who stood in his path, but his quickness gave opponents another worry to consider.

In a 1981 game against Brookwood High, Bo delivered a crunching hit on the quarterback just a split second after he released a screen pass. The force of the collision also dropped Jackson, who scrambled to his feet and chased down the receiver, Atchison said, "for about a three-yard gain."

□

As a high school senior, Bo Jackson was not the polished public personality who today handles an appearance on the Arsenio Hall Show with the same ease he handles a 3-2 fastball.

Bo was trying to overcome a stuttering problem. His confidence away from the playing field was not yet fully fledged. But in one emotional moment in the fall of 1981, Bo's classmates may have matured more due to his one deed than from all of their high school experiences combined.

Like most schools, McAdory High published an annual yearbook. One of the more popular features in the publication was the list that recognized the student most likely to succeed, the most athletic, the best-looking, best-dressed and so on. In the fall of 1981, however, the yearbook staff accidentally omitted several categories from an early draft of the list. One of those categories was "most athletic," which surely would have been awarded to Jackson.

This did not sit well with the school's black students. To protest the omissions, they planned to stage a silent sit-in at a pep rally scheduled the day before McAdory played a pivotal football game.

Coach Dick Atchison brought his football team into a strangely quiet gym that Friday afternoon. Atchison took the microphone and told the students that his team needed to play together, and since the rest of the student body obviously wasn't united, he was removing his team from the gym.

The school principal took action. She assembled the seniors in the library. Blacks sat on one side of the room, whites on the other. Some unkind words were slung back and forth.

One of the seniors who listened to the bickering was Bo Jackson. As the war of words escalated, Bo decided enough was enough and stood up to speak.

"I didn't come to school here to get all the glory and win trophies," he said. "I came here for my education. Ya'll better get your act together right now." And he walked out.

"As soon as he's done," baseball Coach Terry Brasseale said, "everyone starts crying and hugging and kissing each other. It was quite a thing."

Thus ended the unrest. "They respected him that much," Atchison said. "They added those yearbook categories, and Bo got most athletic."

IT GOT SO HE DIDN'T EVEN HAVE TO FIGHT AFTER A WHILE ... HE'D JUST PULL OFF HIS SHIRT AND LET HIS BIG BROTHER PUNCH HIM IN THE STOMACH. HIS REPUTATION BEGAN TO PRECEDE HIM — AND EARNED HIM A LIFELONG NICKNAME —

He's tough like a Wild Boar!

Lahk a Bo'?

BUT BY HIGH SCHOOL HE WAS STILL TOUGH, BUT ONLY ON THE VARIOUS PLAYING FIELDS. THE 'BULLY' HAD BECOME SHY — ALMOST RECLUSIVE — AND THE ONLY STEALING HE DID WAS ON THE BASEBALL DIAMOND —

LITTLE "BO" HAD GROWN UP. AND THE WHOLE WORLD WAS WATCHING ....

THAT'S 90 BASES IN 91 ATTEMPTS!?

SORRY ABOUT THAT OTHER BASE, COACH. I'LL JUST HAVE TO TRY HARDER!?

Go to bed, Bo! There's no agents and college reps around — it's 2:00 in the morning!

I don't know.... I think they're still out there!

A STAR RISES AT AUBURN

Bo Jackson is not supposed to be able to play with pain. That's what his critics say. That's not what Kyle Collins believes.

In the three seasons he played with Jackson in the Auburn backfield, Collins heard the critics take Bo to task for "lying down" on occasion, for taking himself out of key games with injuries. "Whatever happened to being carried off the field," Sports Illustrated mused in a dispatch touting none other than Plymouth State's Joe Dudek for the 1985 Heisman Trophy.

Bad press hardly fazed Bo, but it stuck in Collins' craw. He remembers the Bo Jackson who bit the bullet after Texas' All-America safety Jerry Gray rode him to the ground like a steer in the second game of the 1984 season. Jackson landed hard on the artificial turf, his own weight and Gray's pile-driving his shoulder into the carpet.

"He never said anything about it," Collins said. "He rubbed on his shoulder and shook it around and he played most of the fourth quarter. That was pretty amazing."

Amazing because Jackson had suffered a separated shoulder, an injury that would require surgery and keep him on the sidelines for six weeks. Before Auburn's trainers pulled him out of the game, Bo increased his rushing total to a team-leading 103 yards, not counting a touchdown run that was negated by a penalty.

It mattered not to Bo's detractors, who took particular pleasure when he bowed out of two important games the following season. Jackson had powered his way to an early lead in the race for the Heisman, rushing for more than 200 yards in four of Auburn's first six games. But there was a stain on his record.

At Tennessee in the third game, Bo had removed himself from the lineup with a sprained knee in the third quarter. He stood on the sideline afterward with apparently no medical attention, no ice pack, no heating pad. The ABC-TV cameras even beamed his smiling countenance to a national audience.

By the time Jackson grabbed the pine for good, the No. 1-ranked Tigers were well on their way to a humbling 38-20 defeat in Knoxville. Bo was blamed for being the first one off the sinking ship. He was denounced for not being tough enough.

Against Florida five games later, as Bo sat in the locker room at halftime, memories of those accusations flooded back. His thigh was badly bruised and packed in ice, compliments of a shot from the helmet of Gator linebacker Alonzo Johnson.

As he struggled with the pain, Jackson knew it was beyond the realm of reason to attempt a comeback in the second half, regardless of what was

Bo Jackson's first steps into the national sports scene were taken with football in hand as a talented running back for Auburn University.

Bo really knew football during his four years at Auburn . . .

at stake. Florida entered the game ranked No. 2 in the Associated Press poll, Auburn was No. 6.

Sitting in the small trainers' room, Jackson started to cry. "He had tears in his eyes," recalled student trainer Richard French. "He knew what was coming. He knew the hell he was going to catch."

Jackson didn't emerge from the locker room until 10 minutes remained in the third quarter. He went back in the game for one series in the fourth period, carrying once more for no gain. For the second time that season, Jackson left a game early with an injury. For the second time, Auburn lost.

His totals for the day: 16 carries, 48 yards, one badly bruised thigh, one badly bruised reputation. Sports Illustrated joked that if Jackson won the Heisman, "maybe (Tiger tailback) Brent Fullwood can pick it up for him."

. . . but he also wielded a big bat for the Tiger baseball team.

Auburn Coach Pat Dye seethed over that kind of criticism.

"Nobody knew Bo was walking around on crutches the night after the game and all the next day," Dye said. "They had a sleeve they put his entire leg in. They used ice water and pressure to stop the (internal) bleeding. He didn't fake any injury.

"Bo hasn't ever had to make any apologies."

Jackson could have pleaded his case, but that would not have been Bo Jackson. "It wasn't easy," he acknowledged that December as he accepted the Heisman Trophy. "I had to listen to the criticism people dished out and then go out and prove myself all over again. I think I handled that and didn't let it get to me."

It was a forgiving stance, yet Bo shrugged off the criticism as well as the praise. After his freshman year, when he became the Southeastern

Conference's first three-sport letterman in 20 years (football, baseball and track), Jackson suddenly was being trumpeted as the greatest athlete in SEC history.

"It's not for me to brag about if they say it," Bo said. "I just live with it. Just like if they said I'm the worst, I'd have to live with that."

□

In Alabama, Tide rolls. It's a football tradition that touches the entire state, particularly teen-agers raised in the simple little towns on the out-skirts of Birmingham.

Vincent Edward Jackson might have gone to Alabama and become a football, baseball and track star. "I grew up 'Roll Tide,' " he said. "I had my mind set on going to Alabama."

But that all changed when a Crimson Tide recruiter learned that even as a teen-ager, Bo loved nothing more than a challenge.

Jackson won't forget the Alabama recruiting pitch delivered by long-time Tide defensive coordinator Ken Donahue. According to Bo, Donahue told him up front that he probably wouldn't play much football his first two years but might get a chance to start as a junior. And another thing, Donahue said. If Bo decided to attend Auburn, he'd never beat Alabama.

Years later, Donahue wouldn't confirm or deny Jackson's story.

But Jackson did go to Auburn, he did start as a freshman and he did beat Alabama in both his freshman and sophomore seasons.

Auburn football Coach Pat Dye recalled the extent of his recruiting travels involving Bo:

Dye made one visit to the Jackson household. Bo was doing laundry. Dye asked him where he was going to school. Jackson said Auburn. They shook hands. A few months later, Jackson signed a letter-of-intent to attend Auburn.

Before he was officially signed, sealed and delivered to the Auburn campus, Jackson took the 120-mile trip south from Bessemer, Ala., for the ceremonial recruiting visit.

Still quiet and introspective, Bo took a quick liking to the small town-big school atmosphere, the Tigers' coaching staff and football Coach Pat Dye's assurance that he'd be able to play football in the fall and baseball come springtime. Bo said little about his intentions, however.

"I felt all along he was coming," reasoned Bobby Wallace, the Tigers' secondary coach who recruited the Birmingham area, "but with Bo you never knew what he was thinking. You'd call him on the phone and he was extremely quiet. Mostly, he sat back and listened. Later, we learned that

Auburn football Coach Pat Dye made one visit to Bo Jackson's house in Bessemer, Ala., thus ensuring his team's success for four seasons.

Bo was a relative novice when he began playing baseball at Auburn, re-garding the sport as "something to occupy my time."

was just Bo. But it was pretty frustrating at the time because you couldn't tell if he was listening or not."

For Dye, the prospect of Jackson running the football for Auburn essentially was a done deal. "Bo's a guy who didn't say much, but I got the impression that whatever he did say, you could write it down."

Near the end of the visit, Dye asked Jackson, "Can I count on you coming to Auburn?" Bo said yes. "I never asked him again," Dye said.

□

Having drawn considerable heat in the summer of 1987 for deciding to play professional football as a kind of "hobby" while emphasizing his baseball career, Jackson may have had different priorities as a collegiate sophomore.

In a news release issued by the Auburn athletic department in December 1983, Jackson was hailed as the "premier running back in the South" and described as a man whose hobbies were track and . . . baseball.

But here's the kicker. A year and a half earlier, when Bo spurned an offer from the New York Yankees to accept a scholarship to Auburn, neither baseball nor football took precedence.

"I didn't like the idea of bouncing around the minor leagues for three or four or five years," he said of his decision to turn down the Yankees. "Anyway, I could go to Auburn and run track, which is my favorite sport. . . ."

□

For all of his natural baseball ability, the Most Valuable Player of the 1989 major league All-Star Game wasn't exactly well-schooled in the fundamentals of the game in college.

"Bo was still a relative novice about the game," Auburn Coach Hal Baird remembered.

Jackson admitted in a 1985 interview that baseball was more of a diversionary activity, "something to occupy my time" each spring. After batting .279 in 26 games as a freshman, he skipped his entire sophomore season to concentrate on track. He quit, however, midway through the year after failing to land a spot on the U.S. Olympic team.

Consequently, Bo returned to baseball as a junior, fully intent on giving the sport his best shot.

"He came out late for the team, and a week before the season opened he wasn't starting," Baird said. "Then we said to ourselves, 'He's got to be in there.' I mean, that's how close we came to being known as the coaches who kept Bo Jackson on the bench."

In the latter part of the schedule, an Ole Miss pitcher welcomed Jackson back into the fold by dusting him off several times. When Bo returned to the dugout, Baird explained the situation.

"I don't think initially he realized they were throwing at him," Baird said. "After that first at-bat, I told him. Well, right away he got ticked off. (Auburn football Coach) Pat Dye had told me about a certain look that Bo would get in his eyes. He got that look."

The next time Jackson stepped to the plate, the undaunted Rebel pitcher serenaded Bo with another stanza of chin music with his first delivery. "The next pitch," Baird said, "Bo hit it about halfway up the light tower in right-center field. And it took him about 90 seconds to get around the bases."

□

Auburn assistant football coach Bobby Wallace was uneasy. It was June 7, 1982, the day of major league baseball's amateur draft. That morning, the New York Yankees had drafted Bo Jackson in the second round.

Just months ago, Wallace had signed Jackson to a letter-of-intent to play college football at Auburn. The Tiger assistant still believed Bo intended to honor his Auburn commitment, yet he felt a sudden dread when he thought about how Bo had dazzled professional baseball scouts that spring, cranking 20 home runs for McAdory High to tie a national high school record.

Wallace made tracks to Auburn football Coach Pat Dye's office and broke the news of Jackson's selection by the Yankees. "Coach Dye wasn't as worried as I was," Wallace recalled. "He must have been smarter than me. He told me to go see Bo."

Wallace caught a quick flight to Birmingham and drove to the Jackson household in Bessemer, just southwest of the city. When he discovered Bo wasn't home, his apprehension grew.

"There were all kinds of rumors going around," Wallace said. "Someone said the Yankees had taken him somewhere. I knew Bo wouldn't do anything without talking to his mother. So I waited at the house with her."

Published reports have indicated the Yankees offered Jackson a $250,000 signing bonus. Wallace estimated the figure was more likely $150,000. Either way, it was a lot of money for a family of 10 children supported by a mother who worked as a hotel maid.

But Wallace, because he had recruited Jackson, knew something about his family background. "They weren't desperate for money," he said. "His mother (Florence Bond) always provided for the kids. I knew his mother was a strong influence on him, and she always said she wanted him to get his college degree."

Before long, Bo returned from what had been a walk in the woods to contemplate his future (a page, perhaps, from Robert Frost's "Walking Through Woods on a Snowy Evening"). Wallace reiterated what Auburn could offer him in the way of an education and a football career.

"It wasn't a long, dragged out thing," Wallace said. "He told me that afternoon he was still coming to Auburn. Even then you knew that when Bo told you something, that was the way it was going to be.

"A lot of kids in recruiting are wishy-washy. They'll tell you one thing and tell a coach from another school something totally different. Bo wasn't ever like that. Sometimes he told you things you didn't want to hear. But he always told you the truth."

□

"If Bo had decided to concentrate solely on track," Auburn track Coach Mel Rosen said, "he could have been an Olympic sprinter, even at his size."

Bo flirted with track at Auburn, earning a letter in the sport in both his freshman and sophomore seasons. He qualified both years for the NCAA indoor championships in the 60-yard dash, posting a personal best of 6.18 seconds, and came within four-hundredths of a second of qualifying for the U.S. Olympic trials by covering 100 meters in 10.39 seconds at the 1984 Florida Relays.

Olympic sprinter and Auburn graduate Harvey Glance told one of Bo's coaches that for the first 10 yards out of the blocks, Jackson was the most dominating runner he had faced.

"I think that if I wanted to lose 30 pounds," Bo said, "and become a sprinter and beat Carl Lewis, I could do it."

□

Despite his early (yet fleeting) affinity for track, Jackson set out to address a few football-related matters during his collegiate career.

"My first week in college at Auburn, I set three goals," he recalled in a 1987 interview. "Number one, I'm going to be the best running back in the history of Auburn. Number two, win the Heisman Trophy. Number three, be the first pick in the 1986 draft.

"And once I had accomplished that, I had nothing else to look forward to in football. . . ."

□

It didn't take long for the quiet freshman running back to make an impression on Auburn's starting junior quarterback. Randy Campbell still remembers his first practice with Jackson in August 1982.

Auburn was entering its second season under Coach Pat Dye's wishbone offense and the backfield was largely unsettled. Jackson, a 6-foot-1 block of muscle and power, set up at fullback to take handoffs and fakes from Campbell.

"The first play I tried to hand it to Bo and I barely hit him in the ribs with the ball," Campbell said. "I told coach (Bud) Casey (the running backs' boss) to get him lined up right.

"Well, the next play I hit him in the ribs again. I told coach Casey again to line him up right. I figured he was lining up too close to me.

"Coach told me Bo was lined up right and *I* had to speed up. I'd been at quarterback going on three years and that had never happened to me before."

□

Bo hadn't been at Auburn for very long when he took a ride through Talladega National Forest with a few football teammates and athletic dormitory counselor Rusty Deen.

A deer leaped out of the woods and trotted across the road in front of the car. Deen believed it was the first time Jackson, who would become an avid hunter, had seen a deer in the wild.

Without missing a beat, Jackson exclaimed, "Give me a different pair of shoes and I'll chase that sucker down and catch him."

□

As the Auburn running backs ran through the paces of a routine drill during a routine practice session in 1982, running backs coach Bud Casey smoldered as a freshman back carelessly went through the motions.

The Auburn football staff, in its second year with Pat Dye at the helm, was just beginning to earn a hard-nosed reputation. And Casey, a former tackle at Alabama, wasn't about to let some greenhorn slide by with mistakes on the practice field, even if the freshman was Bo Jackson.

According to two of Bo's backfield partners, Kyle Collins and Tim Jessie, Casey latched onto Jackson's facemask, an attention-getting tactic usually associated with the Frank Kush commando school of coaching. The coach's point made, Jackson seized the opportunity to deliver a message of

It didn't take long for junior quarterback Randy Campbell to realize that Bo Jackson, Auburn's freshman running back, was something special.

his own: "Don't ever grab me like that again."

Casey was never seen repeating the act.

□

Bo Jackson stuttered. He still does, but the problem isn't as noticeable as when he first arrived at Auburn.

Jackson worked with a speech therapist in college to master most troublesome sounds, one of which was saying "I." The therapist suggested that when Bo was asked a question about himself (which became almost an hourly occurrence), he speak in the third person: "Bo does what's best for Bo" or "If Bo's not in it, Bo doesn't care about it."

That habit made Jackson come off as an egocentric to outsiders who didn't know him personally. Not that he paid any attention to his detractors, even those who poked fun at his deliberate manner of speaking.

"Would you rather I talk slow," he once said, "or say 'you know' all the time?"

□

For all of his grandiose achievements on game day, Jackson didn't always do enough to break a sweat at football practice.

In the two years he was Jackson's teammate, defensive tackle Tracy Rocker never once had occasion to tackle Bo in a scrimmage. "You couldn't hit him," Rocker said, alluding to a "hands-off" policy. "And half the time he didn't practice anyway."

Jackson received preferential treatment almost from Day One, although Coach Pat Dye admitted "it went against our grain." Bo set his own practice schedule—even in preseason workouts—and was absent from much of spring practice while he played baseball and ran track.

"I was a little more liberal with Bo," Dye said. "I called all over the country—Georgia, Oklahoma, South Carolina—asking the coaches, 'How do you handle your superstar?' Everybody said they didn't let the guy do anything but polish at practice.

"The way we did it, I guess, was a little uncomfortable for the players and probably some of the coaches, but never to the degree that anybody ever came to me about it. I told the coaches I'd assume the responsibility. I was going to handle it in a manner where he wouldn't be miserable and neither would I."

Bo apparently knew what was best for Bo and his teammates seemed to agree.

"Everybody knows Bo will be there on Saturdays when it counts," fullback Tommie Agee said.

The camera catches baseball and football star Bo Jackson during a leisurely moment on the Auburn University campus.

□

While Bo eventually built a reputation for not attacking practice with the vigor some coaches ideally wanted, the Jackson football legend at Auburn dates back to his very first scrimmage.

Running against the varsity defense, 19-year-old Bo broke tackles, blew past linebackers and flattened defensive backs while averaging nearly 12 yards per carry.

"I'll never forget that first night scrimmage in the stadium when Bo ran wild," secondary coach Bobby Wallace said. "There was electricity in the air. The coaches could feel it and you could see it in the eyes of the players. Everybody knew this guy was something different. Everybody knew this guy was the real thing."

Three weeks later in his first collegiate game, Jackson rushed 10 times for 123 yards and scored two touchdowns in a 28-10 victory over Wake Forest.

□

Despite rushing for 715 yards in his first nine games, despite heading toward all-Southeast Conference recognition, Bo Jackson did not have the time of his life in his first year at Auburn. He was homesick. He was almost painfully shy. He stuttered. He was unprepared for the media blitz, especially in the two weeks leading up to the 1982 season-ending clash against archrival Alabama.

Coming off a poor game against Georgia, Bo wrestled with his emotions during the open week. On Friday night, a week before the showdown in Birmingham, the lonely freshman left for the bus station in nearby Opelika and sat by himself for hours.

"I was depressed, disillusioned with a lot of things," Jackson said. "I guess it was stress. I wasn't mature enough to handle the pressures associated with playing major-college football.

"I decided it wasn't worth it, that I'd be better off if I left Auburn and returned home."

Then Bo thought about his mother, about how elated she had been when he rejected a contract offer from the New York Yankees to pursue an education and athletics at Auburn instead. "My mom raised 10 kids in a three-bedroom house and we never had much money," he said. "She placed a high value on education and doing well later in life."

He let one bus leave the station, and then another.

Bo thought about his friends, some of whom had fallen victim to the temptations of the street. "I thought about how nobody from my neighborhood had done anything special in sports," he said. "I knew if I quit,

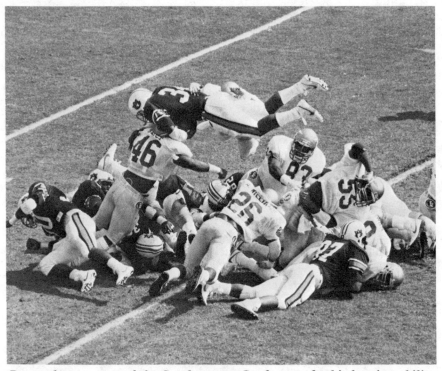

Bo was known around the Southeastern Conference for his leaping ability and penchant for diving over the top.

they'd all be mighty disappointed in me."

Another bus arrived and departed without Jackson, followed by yet another. "Every time one bus would leave, I'd say to myself, 'I'll catch the next one.' But I never did. I just sat there thinking about things."

Midnight came and went. The attendant in charge of the tiny station emerged from his office, ready to leave for the day. "Are you staying or going?" he asked Jackson. "Make up your mind because I'm fixing to close up."

Bo returned to the Auburn athletic dorm. One week later, he scored the diving touchdown (a painting, "Bo Over the Top," commemorates the event) that gave Auburn its first victory over Alabama since 1972.

□

If Bo ran some good times for the Auburn track team, he wasn't always good with time.

During his freshman year, Bo qualified for the NCAA indoor championships after running a time of 6.18 seconds in the 60-yard dash. At the end of the season, the team hopped a bus to Atlanta to catch a plane to Detroit and the championship meet.

"I always tell the kids to go ahead and look around, and they were supposed to meet back (at the airport) at noon," Coach Mel Rosen said. "When it came time to leave, Bo didn't show. There was an Auburn basketball coach sitting in the airport, so I told him to tell Bo to meet us in Detroit."

Four hours later, Jackson rushed into the team hotel in Motor City. Rosen asked why he had missed the original flight.

"He said he was playing video games and forgot about the time change," Rosen said. (Auburn is on Central time; Atlanta, just two hours away by car, is on Eastern time.) "He was just a kid."

Jackson tried to amend for his mistake by following Rosen everywhere—to the restaurant, the gift shop and just about everyplace else the coach turned. Rosen finally asked Jackson why he felt obligated to be his shadow.

"I don't want to miss the next plane," Bo said.

□

When Hal Baird took over as Auburn's baseball coach in 1985, he was continually amazed by Bo Jackson's talent . . . and his inexperience.

"Bo isn't a polished baseball player," Baird observed during preseason practice, "but he's a tremendous athlete. He's one of those athletes you run across once or twice in your lifetime."

Early that year, Auburn traveled to Baton Rouge to take on powerful Louisiana State in a Southeastern Conference doubleheader. Late in the first game, Jackson reached first base with Auburn trailing, 6-0. Bo never needed permission to steal when the opportunity presented itself, but he was subject to a stop sign in certain situations.

This was one of those situations. Jackson didn't run, no rally developed and the Tigers lost, 7-0.

Between games, Baird spotted his cleanup hitter sulking in the corner of the dugout. He asked if there was a problem and Bo acknowledged there was. "I could have stolen that base easy," he said.

Baird agreed but explained the insignificance of one stolen base in the face of a five-run deficit, how the risk outweighed the reward of reaching second. Thus filled with a newfound knowledge of the big inning, Jackson smiled.

"It was like a light bulb went on inside his head," Baird said. "It was amazing some of the things he didn't know that you take for granted from players at this level. But you only had to tell Bo once. After that talk, I didn't even have to give him a stop sign. He knew exactly when it was time to run and when it wasn't."

□

Back in 1982, the Florida Citrus Bowl was known as the Tangerine Bowl, it hadn't cracked the New Year's Day bowl lineup, and the nation was not yet on a first-name basis with Bo Jackson.

Auburn's Tangerine invitation nevertheless marked a resurrection of the school's football program under second-year Coach Pat Dye. The 8-3 Tigers had gained some newfound respect and their first postseason appearance since 1974, thanks in large part to the running of Jackson.

Boston College, led by big-play, small-statured quarterback Doug Flutie, provided the Tangerine opposition. The Eagles' defense knew a little about Bo's reputation, so that each time Auburn quarterback Randy Campbell turned the corner to run the option, a defender sandwiched himself between Campbell and his trailing halfback, thus forcing the quarterback to keep the ball.

Campbell was a capable runner, but he was no Bo Jackson.

"Randy would make a great run," Auburn assistant Bobby Wallace remembered, "and get three yards. Coach Dye started to get upset and called Randy over to the sideline. He told him, 'Dadgum it, pitch the football.'"

With a 17-10 lead, Auburn moved the football to the Boston College 6-yard line. On the ensuing play, Campbell again ran the option—and again found a defender screening his pitch man. Knowing better than to ignore a direct order from Dye, Campbell tossed the ball over the defender's head toward Jackson.

The pitch was too slow for the speeding halfback, but Jackson never broke stride.

"He reached back with one hand," Wallace said, "caught the ball, ran over two guys and scored the touchdown."

Bo finished the game with two touchdowns and the Tigers claimed a 33-26 victory.

□

No matter the opponent, Bo appeared more geared to sack time than game time when the Auburn football team suited up on Saturdays. If he wasn't stretched out sleeping near his locker, Bo probably was drifting around the Tiger locker room with heavy eyelids.

"Before every game I get really sleepy," he said, "like I just took a whole bottle of sleeping pills. But after the first time somebody cracks my head, I'm OK."

□

With each corner Bo turned in his football career at Auburn, his path ran across inevitable comparisons to former Georgia Heisman winner Herschel Walker. One of the earliest came in 1982, when Coach Pat Dye assembled his staff for a progress report on Auburn's list of potential recruits.

As the coaches pitched their respective prospects, Dye's attention was drawn to Vincent (Bo) Jackson, a 220-pound defensive end/running back from McAdory High in McCalla, Ala.

"Coach," assistant Bobby Wallace interjected, "the guy's another Herschel Walker." Like a match set to gasoline, the remark touched off an outburst—of laughter.

As a freshman tailback at Georgia, Walker had led the Bulldogs to the 1980 national championship. As a sophomore in 1981, he set a Southeastern Conference record with 1,891 rushing yards. Jackson had carried perhaps 10 times a game at McAdory and spent as much time playing defense and kicking as he did in the offensive backfield.

"Every coach talks up the guys he's recruiting," Wallace recalled. "It's like being a fan. It's like being a big brother talking about your little brother. So they all laughed at me.

"Everybody was thinking, 'There's only one Herschel Walker.' Well, they were wrong. There was another one out there. I knew it and I think Coach Dye knew it, too."

Like Walker, Bo raced to fame with the No. 34 on his jersey. Both backs were raised in the Deep South, were built along the same lines and had a track man's speed. And while Walker held a decisive edge in most career rushing categories, Bo's average of 6.6 yards per carry (compared with Walker's 5.3 mark) hints at what-might-have-been had he not run his first three seasons under the limitations of Dye's read-and-react wishbone offense.

"When I think of Herschel," Dye would say, "I think of a 10.2 sprinter. When I think of Bo, I think of a 10.3 sprinter who can also high jump 6-10. Bo's just a better all-around athlete."

Jackson elected to shrug off the comparisons. "Nobody is more qualified to be Herschel Walker than Herschel Walker," he noted, "and nobody is better qualified to be me than me."

Pat Dye Jr. had followed in his father's footsteps and gone to school at

Bo Jackson spent much of his college career hearing himself compared to former Georgia star Herschel Walker — another Heisman Trophy winner.

Georgia, where in 1980 he saw Walker stand the Southeastern Conference on its ear and lead the Bulldogs to the national championship. When dad took the head coaching job at Auburn before the 1981 season, Dye switched universities.

"Back then I thought Herschel was like a new invention," Dye said. "Nobody had ever seen anybody that big, that fast, that powerful. He was like a god."

Early in 1982, his father introduced him to another big, fast, powerful football player who planned to attend Auburn that fall. His name was Bo Jackson.

"My dad said, 'This is going to be the next Herschel Walker,'" Dye remembered, "and I laughed hysterically—on the inside, of course. Bo was very shy. He hardly said two words. But after seeing him play for four years, I will go to my grave arguing that Herschel is not in Bo's class."

□

Emotions were running high when the Florida Gators came calling on the Auburn Tigers in 1983. Auburn, fighting for its first Southeastern Conference title since 1957 (and only its second in history), had mustered a 6-1 record and the No. 4 ranking in the Associated Press poll along a schedule mined with dates against Texas, Tennessee, Florida State and Mississippi State. Fifth-ranked Florida, in search of its first-ever SEC crown, had streaked to a 6-0-1 start, its best since 1966.

There was no love lost between the two schools. In the week before the game, Jackson and his teammates labeled the Gators a band of late-hitters and ruffians. Florida Coach Charley Pell accused the Auburn coaching staff of trying to influence officials by criticizing his team's sportsmanship.

Clearly, both schools hadn't forgotten their last meeting, when a disputed fumble ruling late in the game gave Florida possession that led to a game-winning field goal. This season it would be the Gators' turn to cry foul.

With Auburn leading 21-7 in the third quarter, Florida tailback Neal Anderson lowered his head on a goal-line run from the Auburn four. Hit just as he reached the stripe, Anderson fumbled and the ball rolled out of bounds through the end zone. Touchback, the officials decided, ruling Anderson had lost the ball before he broke the plane. Auburn ball at the 20.

On the ensuing play, Jackson cradled a handoff in the backfield and bolted 80 yards for a touchdown that put the game out of reach.

"If the game had been a court case, I don't think it would have ever gone to trial," Pell fumed. "The jury was obviously prejudiced. Any judgment call was going to go against us."

And just how primed had Jackson been to avenge the 1982 loss to Florida?

"He had the flu that day and almost didn't play," recalled Richard French, a student trainer. "Before the game he was throwing up and stuff."

On Auburn's first possession, Bo slashed through the line and dashed 55 yards for a score. He finished the day with 196 rushing yards.

□

Before Bo Jackson arrived at Auburn, nine years had passed since the Tigers last defeated Alabama. They hadn't won a Southeastern Conference title since 1957. By the end of Jackson's sophomore season, Auburn had rolled the Tide twice and won the 1983 SEC championship.

By 1985, Auburn officials did not know whether to promote Bo Jackson as a football or baseball star — so they compromised.

Once past the trials of his freshman season, Bo began to make better use of his abundant gifts. His decision as a sophomore to "deliver the blow rather than take it" was a sensible one, considering the shock he imparted when tacklers collided with his 53-inch shoulders, 46-inch chest and 26-inch thighs.

The net result of his resolution: Bo graduated from All-SEC in 1982 to All-America in 1983, from 829 rushing yards in 1982 to an SEC-leading 1,213 yards in 1983.

□

The Auburn players were somewhat awe-struck as they entered the cavernous Louisiana Superdome to prepare for their 1984 Sugar Bowl date against Michigan. To ease the tension, Jackson and backup quarterback Pat Washington challenged one another to an impromptu throwing contest.

"I've seen Bo throw the ball 80 yards without a warmup," Jack Crowe, Auburn's offensive coordinator, once said. "I heard he could throw it 100 yards, but after 80, everything else is overkill."

Standing on the 50-yard line, Jackson looked up and unleashed a bullet pass that bounced off the Superdome's overhead "gondola," a 75-ton, six-screen television replay board suspended 160 feet above the playing field. Since the facility opened in 1975, only punter Ray Guy, who boomed a space shot off the screens in the 1976 Pro Bowl, has hit the gondola during an actual game, according to Will Penegy, the Superdome's vice president of public relations.

Washington wasn't able to match Jackson's feat but did manage a noteworthy accomplishment of his own. The Tigers' No. 2 quarterback injured his shoulder on his attempt, leaving starter Randy Campbell without a completely healthy backup the following day.

"I had to change my throwing motion," Washington said. "I couldn't throw a 10-yard pass after that."

Washington's arm eventually healed but the damage to his ego lingered. Later that spring, Auburn baseball Coach Hal Baird overheard Jackson and Washington arguing good-naturedly over dinner about who owned the better right arm.

The three left the athletic dining hall for Plainsman Park, Auburn's home baseball field. From home plate, Washington launched a football well into center field, Baird said, about 70 to 80 yards away.

"Bo's throw," Baird said, "hit the base of the fence in center field."

The distance from home plate to dead center in Plainsman Park is 390 feet, or 130 yards.

□

With an outside shot at a national championship, the No. 3-ranked Auburn Tigers drove into Michigan territory to set up what ultimately would be a game-winning field goal in the 1984 Sugar Bowl. Facing a fourth-and-one situation with less than two minutes to play, quarterback Randy Campbell called timeout to talk sideline strategy with the coaches.

Back on the field, Bo carried on a conversation with halfback Kyle Collins.

Jackson: "Kyle, we're probably going to run the sweep. You really need to pick up this block. We got to have it. We've just got to have it."

Collins: "Don't worry, Bo. There's plenty of time left. We'll be all right."

Jackson: "Kyle, there's less than two minutes in the game."

Collins: "What are you talking about? There's 10:53 left."

Collins pointed toward the "10:53" glowing on the scoreboard. It was, indeed, the correct time . . . of day.

"Kyle," Bo scoffed, "get with the program."

□

In the spring of 1984, Jackson devoted his attention to track while his football teammates sweated through the rigors of spring practice. Bo didn't entirely neglect his football obligations—at least, not from a PR perspective.

Before Auburn's annual spring football scrimmage, Bo asked sports information director David Housel about staging a unique 100-yard race at halftime. Jackson would issue a challenge to all the children in the stands and spot them a 20-yard head start. Everyone who finished ahead of Bo would be his guest at dinner.

About 300 kids poured onto the field at halftime that day. They were off and running en masse, but Bo coasted into the end zone at the front of the pack, spared from a dinner tab that might have been delivered to his table in a three-ring binder.

Instead, Jackson signed autographs for every one of his competitors.

"It was all Bo's idea," said Mike Hubbard, Auburn's associate sports information director. "All the kids had a great time."

□

Seven weeks after suffering a separated shoulder in the second game of the 1984 football season, Jackson was back on the field for five carries in Auburn's 24-3 loss at Florida. With a homecoming date against Cincinnati next on the schedule, Coach Pat Dye announced that Bo would start the game at his customary right halfback spot.

Bo quickly became known around college circles for his prodigious home runs and amazing athletic tools.

As the Tigers lined up in the wishbone on their opening series, however, Jackson watched from the sidelines as Kyle Collins started in his stead.

"During our pregame meal," offensive coordinator Jack Crowe said, "I sat with Bo and (assistant) Coach (Larry) Blakeney and we got to talking about some things we wanted to do in the game. Then I got to asking Bo how he felt and how many times did he think he could carry the football. All of a sudden, he looks at me and says, 'Am I starting? Coach, I don't think I should. I think Kyle ought to start ahead of me.'"

As a result, Collins drew one more starting assignment after filling in for Bo the previous seven games, even though Jackson would take over on the second series and rush for 57 yards and three touchdowns on eight carries.

"I'm not surprised at what Bo did because he's that kind of person," said Collins, a transfer from Jacksonville (Ala.) State. "Bo and I are good friends and I guess he just felt, because he's coming back from the injury, that I deserved to start."

□

After his junior season on the diamond, Bo stuck around campus to garner a few summer credit hours. On the way back from class one afternoon, he dropped by Coach Hal Baird's baseball camp for high school prospects.

The Tiger coach had brought out the radar gun that day to get a reading on some of the pitchers. Bo, who had never hummed one through the beam, asked for a shot.

Without a warmup, without spikes, Jackson fogged across three pitches that Baird swears were clocked at 89, 89 and 90 mph.

"And that was on what pro people call the slow gun, the ray gun," Baird said. "If it had been the Jugs gun, it would have been timed even faster, about 93 or 94 mph. Nobody believes that, but we had about 100 campers watching. It was another one of Bo's Herculean feats."

□

When Mississippi State traveled to Auburn in the spring of 1985, the Bulldogs were headed for the College World Series powered by a lineup graced by three future major league stars.

In many ways, the muscular youngster was like a man playing among boys.

First-year Auburn Coach Hal Baird knew that the 50 or so scouts who had assembled in Auburn were there first and foremost to see Mississippi State phenoms Will Clark, Rafael Palmeiro and Bobby Thigpen. But they also wanted a glimpse at a junior Tiger outfielder who happened to play a little football in the fall.

After running track as a sophomore, Bo had rejoined the baseball team and started to realize some of the potential that would soon hold the rapt attention of the scouting fraternity. Based on early contacts, Baird knew the scouts were impressed by Jackson's rare combination of power and speed, but they were less sure of his arm. Bo would square that matter in the finale of the three-game series.

With a runner on second base, Mississippi State's Dan Van Cleave lifted a fly ball to the warning track in center field. "This guy on second tags up against him," Baird said, "and Bo catches the ball in deep center. He doesn't even plant his feet before he throws."

When the runner reaches third base, the ball is already there. "It must have been a 300-foot throw, a bullet," Baird said. "Almost in unison the scouts threw their clipboards in the air as if to say, 'You mean he can do this, too?'"

Bo's storybook throw aside, the Tigers climbed back in the Southeastern Conference playoff picture by sweeping the three-game series—the first time Mississippi State had been swept in an SEC series since 1982. The emotional high for Auburn came in the second game of the series-opening doubleheader, when Bo slammed a game-winning two-run homer in extra innings.

☐

Auburn against Alabama-Birmingham, 1985. Bottom of the eighth inning, the Tigers trailing by one run. Jackson hits what appears to be a routine two-hopper to the shortstop. Bo amazes Coach Hal Baird by "accelerating into another gear" and beating the throw to first.

The next batter hits a home run. Auburn wins, 9-8.

☐

Bo Jackson never needed extra incentive to pay back hated rival Alabama, the school that didn't think he'd be good enough to start until his junior year.

As a freshman, Bo rushed for 114 yards against the Tide and leaped for the game-winning touchdown that terminated Alabama's dominance of the Tigers after nine consecutive victories. The next year, with tornadoes howling through the state, he rumbled for 256 yards and two touchdowns at Birmingham's Legion Field, capping a 23-20 Auburn victory that secured the Tigers' first Southeastern Conference title since 1957.

"When he went over the top (as a freshman) and we beat their damn butts, he became an all-time hero," Auburn publicist David Housel pointed out at the time.

Then came Jackson's junior season. Bo might have gained more notoriety for one play in which he didn't run the ball than for any of his 90 carries that netted 630 career yards against the Crimson Tide.

Bo had put the finishing touch on his sophomore campaign by gaining 130 yards and Most Outstanding Player honors against Michigan in the Sugar Bowl. But before the Tigers could book a return trip to New Orleans in 1985, they had to get past the obstacle posed by Alabama, which already was assured of its first losing record since 1957. Auburn was rated the heavy favorite, but like any other meeting between the cross-state rivals, the game evolved as a pitched battle.

Alabama had mounted a 17-7 lead entering the fourth quarter, but Brent Fullwood's 60-yard scoring run and Jackson's two-point conversion pulled Auburn to within two points midway through the period. On their next possession, the Tigers marched to the Alabama 1-yard line, where they faced a fourth-down situation with 3:44 to play.

Surely, the reasoning went, Auburn Coach Pat Dye, a conservative sort, would opt for the chip-shot field goal and rely on his defense to preserve the lead. If per chance he elected to gamble for the touchdown, surely he'd get the ball to his best back, Bo Jackson.

In came the play from the sideline: a sweep . . . run by Fullwood.

"At first I was surprised we didn't go for the field goal," quarterback Pat Washington recalled. "Then I thought, if we needed only a yard for the touchdown, we were probably going to run a play for Bo."

Jackson also expected to get the ball. "Since we were going for it," he said, "I thought it would be a play to me."

This play would be run to the short side of the field, the *right* side, with Bo and fullback Tommie Agee doing the blocking. When the ball was snapped, Jackson ran *left*. Fullwood, without his lead blocker, ran directly into the Alabama defense. The play lost three yards. Auburn lost a chance for its third straight victory over the Tide.

"I wouldn't have called the damn play if I knew Bo was going to run the wrong way," Dye would say after the game.

Fullwood explained that the play was designated "56 Combo," a sweep to the right. He speculated that Jackson might have believed he heard "57 Combo," which goes to the left.

Whatever the reason, Bo called the mistake the worst of his college career. He dismissed the one touchdown and 118 rushing yards he amassed in just his second start after returning from shoulder surgery. Instead of returning to the Sugar Bowl in New Orleans, Auburn settled for the Liberty Bowl in Memphis.

Bama backers had a field day. They didn't commemorate the upset with a painting, as usual in this series, but with a joke:

"How do you get to Memphis? Go to the 1-yard line at Legion Field . . . and turn left."

□

Atlanta sports agent Pat Dye Jr., the son of Auburn's football coach, remembers watching Bo shoot a round of pool during college.

"I saw him get mad," Dye said. "He got mad and jumped, from a standing start, completely over the pool table sideways. Not from end to end, but from side to side. That was pretty impressive."

□

Foley Field in Athens, Ga., was packed to capacity. More than 3,200 fans had poured through the gates that Tuesday evening in April 1985 to witness the first night game ever played at Georgia. The opposition, Auburn, offered an added attraction with its man for all seasons, Bo Jackson.

Bo was putting together his best season on the collegiate diamond, punishing the ball at a clip that would produce 17 home runs and a .401 batting average. The Georgia fans still knew him better as the man trying to assume the mantle of football fame left behind by their own Herschel Walker.

The Bulldog faithful hounded Jackson before the game, focusing in unfriendly terms on his wrong-way move against Alabama in 1984 that helped keep Auburn out of the Sugar Bowl. Drama was high.

"As usual," Tigers Coach Hal Baird said, "Bo rose to the occasion."

With one out in the fourth inning, Jackson turned on a fastball and crushed a monstrous blast to left-center field. The ball was still climbing when it kissed the top of the new 90-foot light tower, 385 feet away. Some observers claimed the ball would have traveled 600 feet.

"It still was the longest home run I've ever seen an amateur hit," Baird said. "I played against Dave Kingman and I never saw him hit one that far."

Bo belted two more home runs in the game and doubled off the wall in the ninth inning. The crowd booed the last hit.

Taking in the game from the press box, Georgia football Coach Vince Dooley winked at Jackson after watching him ground out to short in the first inning.

After christening the lights with his fourth-inning moon shot, Bo

Bo Jackson put together his best baseball season in 1985, hitting .401 and belting 17 home runs.

looked toward Dooley, who shook his head and laughed. "I'll be glad when that guy goes and plays baseball for good," he told Baird afterward. "I wish he'd go now."

That fall, Bo led the football Tigers to their third straight win over Dooley's Junkyard Dawgs.

□

As the summer of 1985 sweated down toward the start of preseason practice, Jackson was being widely touted as the class of the college football field. Although a separated shoulder had derailed his run for the Heisman Trophy the previous year, Bo was back with a clean bill of health and leading the pack of Heisman candidates.

"I want people to remember me at Auburn by what I do my senior season," he said. "All I'm going to do is step out on the field and be the meanest SOB out there. Everything else after that will take care of itself."

Bo was a hot commodity, and the Atlanta Journal-Constitution asked him to play cover boy for its college football preview, a special issue that would be graced by a full-page photo on the cover. The newspaper's idea people envisioned Bo dressed up in a Superman costume (an "AU" for Auburn replacing the "S"), posing in front of a telephone booth. This was completely out of character for the quiet Jackson, who nevertheless surprised the Auburn athletic staff by agreeing to the photo.

When the day of the shoot arrived, Jackson was by now embarrassed about posing in superhero tights, cape and boots. But, noted Auburn associate publicist Mike Hubbard, "If he gave you his word, you could bank on it."

The phone booth was situated on the corner of Sewell Hall, the Auburn athletic dormitory, thus allowing Jackson to dash from the dorm to the booth as inconspicuously as possible. He made his break, but not quite fast enough to escape detection from a group of workmen passing on a truck.

The truckers hooted at Jackson, who yelled back in mock anger, "You better hush up or I'll fly up there and get you." The workers hushed. Jackson smiled. The photographer snapped the picture. Super Bo was born.

□

Optimism and enthusiasm were heavy in the air as Auburn prepared for the start of the 1985 college football wars. The Tigers, ranked No. 1 in The Sporting News' preseason poll, had hot-rodded their offense by installing a motion-oriented I-formation in place of Coach Pat Dye's read-and-react wishbone.

Dye's trademark offense often had produced more doubts than points during Jackson's first three seasons. The read-and-react nature of the wish-bone frequently kept the ball out of Bo's hands when Auburn could have used him most (see Jackson's seven carries in the lone loss of 1983 season vs. Texas).

Entering his senior year, Bo had averaged just 13 rushing attempts per game and had never carried the ball more than 22 times. That's not exactly taking advantage of a back who had averaged 6.8 yards per run.

"Bo's going to love our new offense," Auburn offensive coordinator Jack Crowe said. "I'm anxious to see him as a tailback. I don't think we've had a chance to see the real Bo Jackson yet."

Jackson, a three-time consensus All-America, would run for a school-record 1,786 yards and win the Heisman Trophy. In Auburn's season-opener against Southwest Louisiana, Bo carried the ball 23 times for 290 yards. He would rush for more than 200 yards in three of the next five games, each time carrying more than 30 times.

□

Bo was a rare physical specimen who maintained his muscle mass through natural exercise rather than weight room sweat. Bo rarely pumped iron, yet he was blessed with the raw strength to walk in off the street and bench press more than 400 pounds.

"He's a genetic phenomenon," Auburn strength coach Paul White marveled. "Whatever he lifts, it's on his own."

□

On October 19, 1985, Bill Curry was trying to do something he'd never done before—and never would in seven seasons as Georgia Tech's football coach. He was trying to beat Auburn.

Curry's 1985 Yellow Jacket team would be his best ever, posting a 9-2-1 record and Tech's lone bowl appearance under his leadership. For most of his tenure, Curry would struggle to uphold Georgia Tech's proud football tradition, but on this October afternoon, forgotten memories of past Tech glories seemed to be revived.

With the fourth quarter fading fast at historic Grant Field, Curry's Rambling Wreck clung to a 14-10 lead as Auburn took over possession deep in its own territory. Facing a key third down from their 24-yard line, the Tigers called a toss sweep to Jackson to the short side of the field.

Bo gathered in the pitch from quarterback Pat Washington, turned toward Tech's "Black Watch" defense and sped through the line. One tackler lined up an angle to deliver the hammer—and Bo accelerated past just inside the sideline. Another defender had the drop to knock Jackson out of bounds—just as Bo gave it the gun in front of Curry on the Tech sideline.

Seventy-six yards later, Bo stopped in the end zone with the winning touchdown.

"One minute he's trotting down the sideline—even when he was running full speed he looked like he was trotting—and the next minute guys with angles were missing him," Auburn tackle Stacy Dunn said. "He kept us from getting our ass beat."

Jackson finished the day with 242 yards rushing, his third-highest collegiate total; Curry saw Tech's record fall to 4-2.

"On the day we played Auburn," Curry said, "Bo Jackson was the best I've ever seen in college football."

☐

It was hush-hush all week. The pain was nature's way of telling Bo something was wrong. But he remained silent.

Four days before his last regular-season collegiate football game, four days before Alabama, Jackson finally went for an X-ray that revealed one cracked rib and another broken clean in two. The damage had been done by the Georgia defense during the previous game, a 121-yard, two-touchdown performance that may have ultimately sealed the Heisman Trophy for Auburn's all-time rushing leader.

Yet if Bo missed another big game because of injury, the national press would know no pity. In the week leading up to Alabama, Sports Illustrated hit the stands with a cover story that argued Jackson didn't have the right stuff for the Heisman, that in big games he "grabs more bench time than Sandra Day O'Connor."

No one would let him forget that he had come out of the Tennessee game with a sprained knee and the Florida game with a bruised thigh. Two injuries, two early exits meant two Auburn losses.

But Bo Jackson was born to play against Alabama. The Auburn football staff had to protect those ribs, however, and someone brought up the idea of a flak jacket. "Bo didn't like that," equipment manager Frank Cox said. "Plus, you wear one of those things, you're just advertising."

Advertising would not work. If the Tide defense detected Jackson was wearing special protection, he'd be one inviting target. The Tigers would not leak word of the injury until they informed the ABC-TV announcers just before game time.

Instead of a flak jacket, the coaches reasoned, why not a special pair of shoulder pads, "longer in the back to cover up where those ribs were

Bo's best football season was 1985, when he rushed for 1,786 yards and 17 touchdowns while garnering enough votes to win the Heisman Trophy.

broken," Cox said. The problem was finding an equipment company that could manufacture the pads on such short notice.

Auburn found that company in Leeds, Ala. Three days before the game, Cox paid a visit to Vulcan Athletics and waited while the pads were constructed. "You wear one of those things," Cox said, "and you don't even know there's anything (under) there."

Thus cloaked—in padding and in secrecy—Jackson played against Alabama. He rushed for 142 yards, caught two passes for 25 yards and scored two touchdowns.

He also set records. Bo's 17 rushing touchdowns and 102 total points established single-season school marks. He set another with 1,786 yards rushing, second in Southeastern Conference history to the 1,891 yards gained by Georgia's Herschel Walker in 1981.

"We wanted to keep the injury low all week so the other team wouldn't try to get to him as much," Auburn tackle Steve Wallace said. "If anybody goes out there and plays with two broken ribs, if that's not courage, what is? I respect him as much as you can respect a person."

Jackson's gutsy performance wasn't enough to prevent Van Tiffin's last-second 52-yard field goal and Auburn's second straight loss to Alabama.

"It's like you're at the top of a ladder," Jackson said, "and at the last step before you get to the top, somebody pulls the ladder from under you."

The ribs would mend, but the controversy around Bo would not cease. After reading of Jackson's courageous performance against Alabama, an astute newspaper reader in Birmingham pondered a photo that had appeared in the Birmingham Post-Herald on game day. The picture showed Bo's Auburn teammates playfully carrying him on their shoulders during a Friday walk-through at Legion Field.

Why would someone with cracked ribs be hoisted like a rifle on the day before Auburn played its biggest rival, the reader wondered. Were the "cracked ribs" nothing more than a publicity stunt to gain sympathy and Heisman votes for Jackson, who had been maligned throughout his senior season for a low pain threshold?

The Birmingham News sent a reporter to investigate. At a hospital clinic in Auburn, he looked firsthand at Jackson's X-rays. Indeed, one rib was broken through and a second cracked. The writer talked to the team doctor and filed his story.

A week later, Bo and the reporter took the same flight from Atlanta to New York for the Heisman Trophy announcement. The ticket agent at the Atlanta airport recognized Bo and bumped him from coach to first class, where he could escape the entreaties of common people and the press.

At La Guardia Airport, Jackson finally came face to face with the reporter and smiled. "So how did you like my ribs?" Bo wondered.

□

Bo's last great act on a collegiate football field was symbolic of his bittersweet final two years at Auburn.

Playing with two cracked ribs against Texas A&M in the Cotton Bowl, Jackson rushed for 129 yards (his 23rd 100-yard game at Auburn), caught two passes for 73 yards and was named the game's top offensive player. He scored touchdowns on a five-yard run and a 73-yard screen pass that was classic Jackson.

With the game on the line in the fourth quarter, however, it was the

Auburn's prized tailback poses with the Heisman Trophy at New York City's Downtown Athletic Club.

Aggie defense that hunkered down and stonewalled Bo. On fourth-and-goal at the A&M 2-yard line and again on fourth-and-two at the Aggie 27, Bo was stuffed for one-yard losses.

After bowl victories in each of Bo's first three seasons, Auburn went home a loser, 36-16. Moreover, the loss dropped the Tigers' final record to 8-4, their worst during the Jackson era.

□

The 1985 Heisman Trophy announcement was a couple of days and about 1,000 miles away. Bo Jackson, Auburn tailback, would make the trip to New York City's Downtown Athletic Club. But this particular day would begin in the library of Auburn's athletic dormitory, where Bo had a date to meet the press.

Someone else also was there to meet Jackson, however. Bo spotted him on the couch right away when he entered the interview room. Rusty wasn't a reporter. He was there with his mother, father and younger brother from Decatur, Ala. Rusty was 11 years old. He had leukemia. It was his wish to spend the day with Bo Jackson.

Jackson excused himself from the media and took Rusty to his dorm room, where he presented the boy a baseball cap and an Auburn sweatshirt. Downstairs, reporters were asking questions about the boy. They discovered he needed money for a bone marrow transplant.

That evening, the story became public and the money started coming in.

But that day is what Peggy England remembers most about Bo Jackson. She is the founder and director of Gifts Inc., a Birmingham, Ala., group that grants wishes to chronically and terminally ill children and victims of child abuse.

Bo, Rusty and his younger brother spent the afternoon bumming around town. Part of the day involved eating ice cream and picking out remote-control cars at the Auburn mall. A better part of their time was spent racing the cars around the offices at Memorial Coliseum.

"I never asked Bo to do those things," said England, who arranged the visit with help from Auburn associate sports information director Mike Hubbard. "I just asked him to meet the little boy. Bo really cared."

When Rusty went to Seattle for his marrow transplant, Bo called him in the hospital the night before the operation. Afterward, Rusty returned to Children's Hospital in Birmingham, where Jackson popped in for a visit.

Rusty died within months, but the memory of his day with Bo lives with England, who has since called on Jackson to grant a similar wish.

"In public, Bo may sometimes seem arrogant," England said. "But that's not really him. I think he's one of the most wonderful people I've ever met in my life. He's my hero."

A few months before meeting Rusty, Jackson made another youngster's dream come true in Oxford, Ala.

Fourteen-year-old Jon Greenwood was in a state of depression, his weight and spirits declining after doctors amputated his right leg. He had been critically injured when a car struck him down as he rode his bicycle.

The boys's dietician, an Auburn graduate, was able to get Jon to start eating only after making a deal that she'd obtain the autograph of his hero, Bo Jackson.

Bo received a letter from the woman and decided to come to the boy's emotional rescue. One Friday morning, as Jon sat in a wheelchair under his carport, Bo Jackson walked up his driveway, bigger than life.

"That was totally Bo's own doing," Hubbard said. "He's the one who decided to go up there."

Jackson talked with Jon for more than half an hour, about football, fishing and anything else to lift his spirits. "I knew I had to come down and give him a little motivational talk," Bo said, "just to say life ain't over. . . . I think he knows I care."

□

He was struggling with his game and his decision. On the diamond, Jackson had fanned 30 times in 69 at-bats and was batting .246 in his final year at Auburn. Off the field, he had to make up his mind about his future. Would the nation's most talented amateur athlete pursue a career in pro football or baseball?

In most baseball scouting circles, Bo was regarded as the hottest prospect in the upcoming June 1986 draft. He was far from polished, but his wealth of natural talent far outweighed the imperfections that might have otherwise hindered his potential.

On the other hand, the National Football League draft would be held on April 29, and Jackson, the 1985 Heisman Trophy winner, was expected to be picked first overall by the Tampa Bay Buccaneers.

On March 25, Jackson boarded the private jet of Bucs Owner Hugh Culverhouse to fly to Tampa for a physical examination required by the NFL team. That plane ride ultimately cost Bo the rest of his collegiate baseball career.

Jackson's adviser at the time said Tampa Bay had assured him the trip was not in violation of Southeastern Conference rules. Indeed, the trip itself was within bounds, but a flight paid for by a third party in effect made Jackson a football professional under SEC rules.

"It was an honest mistake," Jackson said. "If I had known it would jeopardize my eligibility, I would never have gone."

Brokenhearted, Bo voluntarily gave up the rest of his season rather than seek to have his eligibility restored.

"I didn't want to go through the red tape and get the team and the coaches involved," he said. "It would be a distraction and they might not perform as well on the field."

The incident so disturbed Jackson that when he was informed he had terminated his amateur status, "he cried like a baby," sports information director David Housel said. "Don't ever say he's not a team player."

Bo was in a more candid mood when he discussed his trip to Tampa in a 1987 interview.

"I had some people . . . some conniving people that tried to get me to sign with Tampa before the (NFL) draft date. They were really pressuring me. The way I see it, if I had signed with Tampa early, the person who was working with me at the time would have gotten a big cut for me signing early. . . .

"I believe he and everyone else in Tampa knew that I was going to be ruled ineligible for baseball when I took that plane ride to see them. Before I got on that flight, I sat down and talked to them and said, 'Did you all check with the SEC, the NCAA, to see if this is all right?'

"They said, 'Yes, we called the office and got permission from the head guy at the SEC. Well, not the head guy because he was out of town, but the guy who was in charge. Yeah, everything's OK.'

"Well, a couple of days later I get back to Auburn and they said it wasn't OK. I think he knew all along what was going on. I think he was in there for his own selfish reasons to make some money."

□

"Maybe I'll take these two pieces of paper and write 'baseball' on one and 'football' on the other and let someone pull one out of a hat."
— Bo Jackson, speculating on a career decision in 1985

Whether he played professional baseball or football, Jackson was going to command a big price in either market. Consequently, Bo wasn't hung up on money as he weighed the advantages of each sport.

"How good can I be in baseball? The sky's the limit," he said before his final season at Auburn. "All it takes is practice. I think I can step into the majors right now and play.

"I just love the game. It's one-on-one with the pitcher when you are hitting and one-on-one with the hitter when you are on defense and one-on-one with the pitcher when he hits you and you go after him.

"In football, once I get the ball, it's 11-on-one. In baseball, it's concentration. In football, in my case, it's more instinct and fear. Fear of the defense.

"It's like living my childhood bully days all over. I can go out there and run over people and bang people and stomp on people and it's not illegal. I can bang heads all day in games, I can go as long as the lights are on in the stadium.

"But on Monday through Thursday, for practices, I'd rather be fishing."

□

It was just another lazy summer day in August 1985. The start of preseason football practice was still a week away. This was a day for fishing.

Bo and two of his closest friends on the football team, fullback Tommie Agee and tailback Tim Jessie, grabbed their gear and hightailed it to their favorite country fishing hole. "Bo and Tim were in the boat," Agee recalled, "and I was fishing from the bank."

As Jackson tended to the business of baiting his hook, Jessie reached back to throw out his first cast.

"The next thing I heard," Agee said, "was *'OUCH!'* "

Agee and Jessie looked quickly at their companion. Bo sat unbelieving in the back of the boat, Jessie's lure stuck in the side of his head.

"It looked like a big earring," Jessie mused.

Jessie and Agee thought the mishap hilarious, as did everyone else at the East Alabama Medical Center in Opelika, where they took Bo to have the lure removed.

"Tim broke his rod and everything," Agee said. "We had to go to the emergency room to get them to cut it out. Everybody that came in there was laughing."

Everyone but Jackson, who winced at the mention of the incident a few days later, his stitches still in place.

"It was my best catch ever," Jessie said. "A 220-pound bigmouth bass."

OH, THERE WAS TALK TO THE CONTRARY. CRITICS WHO SAID HE COULDN'T PLAY WITH PAIN ... _SPORTS ILLUSTRATED_ COMPLAINING THAT HE NEVER EXITED A GAME ON A STRETCHER ... 'BAMA FANS WHO WERE JEALOUS ... AND FOOTBALL FANATICS WHO CONSIDERED HIS DEDICATION TO THEIR FAVORITE SPORT OVER BASEBALL SUSPECT ... BUT, COME HEISMAN TROPHY VOTING TIME ....

THERE WAS LITTLE DOUBT WHOSE FACE WAS ON IT.

...NOT BAD FOR A GUY WHO COULD HAVE PASSED UP COLLEGE BALL ALTOGETHER!

BASEBALL
IN MEMPHIS

T he offer on the table from the Tampa Bay Buccaneers reportedly called for $7.6 million over five years. Oh, the figures might have varied a bit depending upon the source. But one thing was undeniable: The Buccaneers, in their quest to sign the No. 1 selection in the 1986 NFL draft, were prepared to park a truck near the drive-in window of the local bank to meet Bo Jackson's demands.

There was another offer under consideration, one that was being paid little heed by the media and other onlookers because (a) it paled in comparison with that extended by the Bucs and (b) it had been extended by a *baseball* team.

Bo, the reigning Heisman Trophy winner, weighed his options, then made his decision.

"I went with what is in my heart," Jackson said on June 21, 1986.

To the amazement of most people and the consternation of many, Jackson uttered the B-word.

"My first love is baseball," he continued, "and it has always been a dream of mine to be a major league player. My goal now is to become the best baseball player that Bo Jackson can be."

It was disclosed that Jackson was signing a three-year, $1.06 million contract with the Kansas City Royals, who had made him a fourth-round draft pick earlier in the month.

While disbelieving souls shook their heads, Royals General Manager John Schuerholz played it cool. Or rather cool, anyway.

"It's not a surprise that we signed him," Schuerholz said. "The surprise factor was eliminated when we drafted him. We had information that led us to believe that we had a chance of signing him. We knew what he could do on the field. He can throw, run, field, hit and hit with power. Our scouting evaluation is that he can be a superstar. That's not putting any undue pressure on him. That's what our reports say.

"It's still amazing. The sports world has to be shocked. Jackson left millions of dollars on the table to sign with us. . . ."

How tough was the football-or-baseball decision for Bo Jackson?

"I woke up one morning last week and I was leaning toward baseball," he said. "Then I woke up the next day and I was leaning toward football. That went on day after day. Finally, I sat down and asked myself, 'What am I going to do?' The answer to that question is that I'm standing here (at Royals Stadium, for the news conference announcing his plans)."

One of Bo Jackson's sports idols was Reggie Jackson, who in 1986 was with the California Angels and playing his next-to-last season of major

Bo Jackson, following "what is in my heart," dons a Royals baseball cap and announces that he is spurning the riches of pro football at a June 21, 1986, press conference.

league ball.

Bo said he had sought out advice from Reggie before the '86 baseball draft, and that the noted slugger had helped steer him toward a career on the diamond.

"I've always followed Reggie, and whatever team he was on was my favorite team," Bo explained on the day he signed with the Royals. "I probably wouldn't be standing here today if it weren't for him.

"Now it's time to stop idolizing Reggie and make my own footsteps."

"What sold him on the Royals wasn't anything that was said or done the last few days. What sold Bo was what happened to our organization between 1968 and 1986—who we are, what we did, the reputation we've earned. He was sold on the Royals and what we stood for."

—Kansas City General Manager John Schuerholz

"My strengths are my speed and arm. I need to work on hitting the curveball. That's all I need to work on."

—Bo Jackson, after signing with the Royals

"To be frank, I never saw anyone in pro baseball who has the total package he has. Willie Wilson doesn't have his power or his arm. George Brett can't run with him. It's almost unfair. If God were to create a perfect player, how could he change?"

—Hal Baird, Auburn baseball coach
and onetime pitcher in the Royals' farm system,
describing prize pupil Bo Jackson

"He's got superhuman-like skills. No one's been timed faster than him in football (4.12 seconds in the 40-yard dash). He has more power than anyone in baseball (17 homers in 42 games as an Auburn junior). He's got a good arm. And his body looks like it's been chiseled out of a mountain."

—The Royals' John Schuerholz,
summing up the attributes of the newest
player in his organization, Bo Jackson

□

Two other big-league baseball teams, the New York Yankees and the California Angels, had opportunities to sign Bo Jackson. Neither had the right stuff, however.

The Yankees chose Jackson, fresh out of high school, in the second round of the amateur free-agent draft of 1982. The Angels picked him in the 20th round three years later.

". . . When the Yankees drafted me out of high school, I never came close to signing with them," Bo recalled. "I never let them talk to me. I didn't want any part of it.

"I figured, now what would (I) do with a quarter of a million dollars right out of high school? I've never seen that much money in my life, never seen a quarter of that much money in my life. And I'd be moving from a small town, where the tallest building is a 10-story courthouse, to New York.

"I said, 'No way,' simply because I had a scholarship to college, and I could play football, baseball and track all at the same time. Plus, I could get my degree."

Added Bo: "I just don't take too kindly to the Hugh Culverhouses or the (George) Steinbrenners, or folks like that. That's because they think that they can buy a person, and they can put a handle on you, like 'you're

Wearing a major league uniform for the first time on the day of his Kansas City signing, Bo is introduced to cheering Royals fans before being assigned to Class AA Memphis.

my property.' And I refuse to be somebody else's property."

Suffice to say, Tampa Bay Buccaneers Owner Culverhouse and Yankees Owner Steinbrenner were not in the running for Jackson's services.

The Angels weren't, either.

If Bo had indicated an interest in the California club in '85, Angels official Larry Himes says the athlete would have been offered "the richest contract any draft choice has ever received. We wanted to make it worth his while to give up football and say, 'Yes, I will commit myself to baseball the rest of my life.' "

But Jackson, eager for another full year of college life on and off the athletic field, never gave the Angels the time of day.

□

After signing with Kansas City in 1986, Bo Jackson spent time working out with the Royals before getting a ticket to the club's Class AA farm team in Memphis.

In his first batting-practice session at Royals Stadium, Bo hit two cannon shots—balls that landed at the base of the scoreboard in center field, 50 feet beyond the 410-foot marker. A dozen of his drives left the ballpark.

"Well, he has pop in the bat. We've established that," cracked Royals batting coach Lee May.

"I've never seen a ball hit that far in this park," Royals second baseman Frank White said of Bo's first mammoth batting-practice smash in June 1986. "But the thing that really impressed me was the height on that ball. In fact, everything about this day is beginning to impress me."

White knew a little bit about the history of Royals Stadium. He joined the Royals in 1973, the year the Kansas City club moved into the sparkling facility.

"He doesn't swing like a football player to me."
—The Royals' Hal McRae,
one of the most respected hitters
in the American League for more than a decade,
after his first look at Bo Jackson in the batting cage

□

"I could have played football. I could have signed a contract and become an instant millionaire. You all can say anything, but I'm trying to make a living. This is the first day of summer and summer's a time for baseball, and I'm ready to go.

Bo's arrival in Memphis required another press conference and more questions about his decision to play baseball instead of football.

It was get-acquainted time for Bo Jackson on June 30 as he mingled with Chicks teammates before making his professional baseball debut.

"This is what Bo wants to do the rest of his life. . . ."
                     —Bo Jackson, the day he cast his lot with the Royals

"Once I signed on the dotted line (with the Royals), I knew I would never play football again. I've had my share of football. Not to brag, but I've got my trophy."

                                     —Heisman winner Bo Jackson, June 1986,
                                        telling Kansas City reporters that he was a
                                        baseball player now and forever more

                                     □

When Bo Jackson opted for professional baseball over pro football in 1986, he made big news. Really big news.

After all, Jackson had been the No. 1 selection in the entire '86 National Football League draft. Plus, six months before saying yes to the Kansas City Royals' organization, he had been awarded college football's most-treasured prize, the Heisman Trophy.

Still, Bo chose baseball—and he made his debut as a professional athlete on June 30, 1986, with the Royals' Class AA farm club in Memphis. The game, which matched Jackson and the Chicks against Columbus, may have been the most publicized minor league contest in history.

A Chicks official said "well over 200" members of the media were on hand at Tim McCarver Stadium in Memphis. Out-of-town newspapers and magazines represented included The Sporting News, Sports Illustrated, Newsday, Chicago Tribune, Los Angeles Times, Dallas Morning News, Atlanta Constitution, (New Orleans) Times-Picayune, Cincinnati Post, Kansas City Star, Dallas Times-Herald, People, USA Today, Philadelphia Inquirer, Washington Post and Detroit News.

ABC, CBS and NBC also were there, as were many print and electronic outlets from Jackson's home state of Alabama, his would-be home base of Florida (had he chosen to play with the NFL's Tampa Bay Buccaneers) and his temporary home state of Tennessee.

"It was like a Miss America pageant," said Ted Tornow, the Chicks' director of media and public relations. "You know when they say 'electricity is in the air'? That was it. You didn't know what he was going to do."

There was electricity in the air as game time neared for the Kansas City Royals' heralded farmhand.

Jackson had played less than 2½ baseball seasons at Auburn. Prior to signing with the Royals three weeks into June, Bo had last played competitive baseball in March (for Auburn). Skeptics doubted his ability to hit professional pitching, especially the curveball.

With the national media recording his every move and the crowd chanting, "Go, Bo, Go," Jackson stepped to the plate in the first inning for his first professional at-bat—and proceeded to bounce a single up the middle against Columbus righthander Mitch Cook. The hit drove home a run, giving the Chicks a 3-0 lead. The ball was thrown over to the Memphis dugout as baseball milestone No. 1 for Jackson, but Bo said it wasn't a keeper.

"I have enough balls in my trophy case," Bo said. "After I get a hit in Kansas City—if I get there—I'll keep that ball."

Asked about Jackson's mechanics at the plate when Bo began his professional baseball career with the Class AA Memphis Chicks in late June of 1986, Ken Berry, minor league batting instructor for the parent Kansas City Royals, said: "I like what he's doing."

Then Berry added: "I've been told my body will be in the river if I mess with him too much."

Memphis Manager Tommy Jones couldn't contain his enthusiasm over Bo's first trip to the plate in a Chicks uniform.

"It looked like something out of 'The Natural,' " Jones said. "To fight off pitches and get a two-out hit in his first at-bat was something to remember."

Jackson went hitless in his final three at-bats that night, striking out twice. But he had made quite a first impression.

□

Bo Jackson's impact on the Memphis Chicks and the Southern League was immediate and indelible.

One Memphis hotel, which never had done business with the Chicks, called the team before Jackson's first game and offered some complimentary rooms for members of the national media in town to cover Bo's debut.

Large crowds of fans and reporters began to show up wherever Jackson and the Chicks went. On his first stop at each league city, Jackson could not leave the ballpark immediately after a game with the rest of the team. The crush of admirers was particularly evident in Birmingham and Huntsville, Alabama cities where Bo had built a large following during his Auburn days.

"Everybody wanted an autograph," Chicks publicist Ted Tornow said. "We'd let the rest of the team go. The visiting-team clubhouse manager and I would wait an hour or an hour and a half while Bo signed every autograph. I gained a lot of respect for him right there."

Tornow also lost a lot of sleep playing liaison between Jackson and the media.

Despite the pressure created by a big media assault, Bo still found time to clown during outfield drills prior to his first minor league game.

□

Everywhere Bo Jackson went in his tour of the Southern League, people wanted to know why he gave up football. Would he ever play football
again? What made a football player think he could play baseball?

This, of course, was before the days in Kansas City when Jackson laid
down the law that he would talk only about baseball during baseball
season, football during football season and hunting and fishing the rest of
the time.

Bo didn't always respond directly to the queries. Sometimes, he simply
let his actions give some hint as to what was going on in his mind.

A case in point: The Memphis Chicks were playing in Charlotte. Jackson was in the on-deck circle when a fan stood up and fired a tiny plastic
football in his direction. The stadium erupted in laughter, and Jackson
joined in the spirit of the occasion.

Bo picked up the ball, tossed it around and then decided to keep it. He
carried the ball everywhere on the road swing—to the pregame press conference set up on his first day in a new town, to the outfield before games
(at which time he would play catch with teammates), sometimes to the
outfield during games (at which time he would play catch with the ballboy
between innings) and on the team bus.

□

Some athletes rise to the occasion in dramatic-yet-laid-back style.
Others do it with a flair. Count Bo Jackson in the latter category.

The Memphis Chicks were batting in the bottom of the ninth inning in
a tie game with the Greenville Braves. The bases were loaded and Jackson
was at the plate.

Bo fouled off one pitch, and another, and then another.

Then, in the words, er, word, of Chicks publicist Ted Tornow,
"BOOM!"

Tornow recalled what transpired.

"He hit the longest ball in our ballpark anyone could remember,"
Tornow said. "When it left the park, it was already in the lights and it was
still going up. It was like a 5-iron."

One of the clubhouse attendants saw the ball land, and the next day
the smash was measured at 554 feet.

"It had to be right at 600 feet," Greenville Manager Jim Beauchamp
insisted. "The last player I saw hit one that far was Frank Howard."

While Bo Jackson hit his first professional home run at Charlotte, it
was another homer he hit there that really grabbed attention. It was a

gen-u-ine jaw-dropper.

Jackson swung and, according to Tornow, "you could hear his bat crack . . . I'm not talking splinter. I'm talking crack. The ball sailed over the 400-foot sign. He was like a man playing against boys."

☐

At Auburn, Bo Jackson played in a total of 89 baseball games—a number that a big-league regular will approximate by the time the All-Star break rolls around.

Accordingly, did the sages take a conservative wait-and-see approach as football star Bo prepared to make the transition to professional baseball in the summer of 1986? Consider the opinions of three baseball men:

Tommy Jones, Jackson's manager at Memphis: "I swear I'm looking at Ted Williams. He's got Hall of Fame numbers on his scouting report."

Ewing Kauffman, co-owner of the Royals: "He could be greater than George Brett. He has more speed and power. Why, he could easily be another Mickey Mantle or Willie Mays."

Larry Himes, then director of scouting for the California Angels: "You don't see this kind of talent come along very often. He has Jim Rice-kind of power and Willie Wilson-type speed. He's a strength-and-speed guy, like Kirk Gibson, but he's stronger and bigger and has a better arm than Gibson. He could have an effect on baseball like Mickey Mantle or Willie Mays, and he's bigger and faster than either of them."

"I have to laugh when I hear these people comparing him (Bo) to Jose Canseco," said one American League scout who wished to remain anonymous.

"Come on, there's no comparison. Canseco doesn't have a thing on this guy.

"I'll tell you what. I don't think he's a football player playing baseball. I think he's a baseball player playing football."

Hugh Alexander, who played briefly in the major leagues before suffering the loss of a hand in an off-season accident, has been scouting ballplayers for more than 50 years. He has seen Babe Ruth and Lou Gehrig play. He has scrutinized Willie Mays and Mickey Mantle. He has analyzed Roberto Clemente.

"I've been watching this game for so long that everybody always asks me, 'Who are the best ballplayers you've ever seen?' " said Alexander, who now works for the Chicago Cubs. "I always tell them the same four: Babe Ruth, Joe DiMaggio, Roberto Clemente and Willie Mays.

"Right away, people ask, 'Hey, how about (Stan) Musial? How about

(Hank) Aaron?' I tell them when I started doing scouting, I learned that the really great ballplayers can beat you five different ways: Throwing, running, fielding, hitting and home runs. Only the great ones can excel in all of those phases.

"Now I tell you what, I may have to be adding another name to that list pretty doggone soon. His name's Bo Jackson."

□

"Get it right," a veteran baseball man said as he assessed the baseball aspirations of the former collegiate football star. ". . .He has power, speed, a great arm and a willingness to listen to his elders—but he still has an awful lot to learn."

The young man, coming off an All-America season in which he had rushed for more than 1,000 yards, was attempting to go directly from the campus to the high minor leagues without missing a beat. Furthermore, he was trying to make the big jump with the baseball season well under way—a tough way to break in, to be sure.

The righthanded-hitting outfielder struggled at the outset when he broke into the minors, then came on strong and finished with creditable numbers.

Bo Jackson, 1986, right?

Wrong.

Jackie Jensen, 1949.

The athletic careers of the two-sport standouts contain some striking parallels. Jensen, as a senior, sparked California into the Rose Bowl and reeled off a 67-yard touchdown run in the Pasadena classic; Jackson, as a senior, led Auburn into the Cotton Bowl and was on the receiving end of a 73-yard TD pass play in the Dallas game; Jensen entered pro baseball in '49 at the Class AAA level and, after a difficult start, wound up with a .261 batting average and nine home runs for Oakland of the Pacific Coast League; Jackson made his debut in '86 in the Class AA ranks and, after a horrendous beginning, finished with a .277 average and seven homers for Memphis of the Southern League; Jensen, in his first look at big-league pitching, batted a woeful .171 in 70 at-bats for the 1950 New York Yankees; Jackson, in his first test in The Show, hit .207 in 82 at-bats for the '86 Kansas City Royals.

Could football sensation Jensen really cut it in baseball? Would Saturday hero Jackson measure up in the majors?

Jensen's fate is now a matter of historical record—and some record it is. Bo would do well to rival Jackie's performance—and he seems capable of doing just that. At the very least.

Jensen, traded to Washington and then to Boston, developed into one of the great run-producers in the American League. In one six-season span (1954 through 1959), he drove in 667 runs for the Red Sox. In 1958, he was named the American League's Most Valuable Player.

Jackson, at age 26, walloped 32 homers and knocked in 105 runs for Kansas City in 1989. Jensen's first 100-RBI season came when he was 27 years old, and the Boston slugger didn't attain the 30-homer plateau until he was 31.

□

There's little doubt that Bo Jackson is the best athlete in the majors today, but it was that very multifaceted talent that turned off many big-league scouts in 1986 — and earlier as well.

Only two previous consensus All-America running backs, Sam Chapman and Jackie Jensen, evolved as top-drawer baseball players. Chapman, an All-America at California in 1937, belted 20 or more home runs in a season five times for the Philadelphia Athletics. Jensen, also an All-America at Cal (1948), drove in more than 100 runs in a season five times for the Boston Red Sox.

While Chapman and Jensen did well in the big leagues, the fact

Two-sport standout Jackie Jensen was a senior at the University of California when this 1949 photo was taken.

they represented a distinct minority cast doubt on Jackson's ability to make the football-to-baseball transition with any kind of impact.

Plus, there was a fat contract offer on the table from the Tampa Bay Buccaneers, who had made Bo the No. 1 selection in the 1986 National

Football League draft. How was major league baseball going to compete with the NFL's big bucks?

"It would have been easy to write him off and say he's going to play football," said Kansas City scout Ken Gonzales, the man who kept close tabs on Bo during his Auburn days. "In fact, when scouts came around his senior year, they really were convinced of that. Bo had a lot on his mind and wasn't playing anywhere near his potential.

"A lot of scouts were saying, 'Look at him. He doesn't want to play baseball. He's got football on his mind. Hell, he's not even running too good anymore.'

"I'll remember this one incident for the rest of my life when this scout comes up to me and says, 'I'll tell you right now, he's not going to play baseball. You're wasting your time. But for argument sake, let's say he does. He'll never make it. He'll struggle in rookie league, and it'll take him two years to get out of there.' "

Plenty of other skeptics were sounding off as Bo weighed his professional future. Among them:

Minnesota Twins scout Fred Waters: "He's got Mickey Mantle-type power, but he's got some catching up to do, too, and not only with the bat. He's really not a good outfielder, but his speed was so good in college that it didn't really matter. I'd say he's three or four years away from being able to hit in the big leagues."

Oakland Athletics scout Dick Bogard: "It would take him a number of years in the minor leagues—I don't know, maybe three or four—just for him to learn how to play the game."

Former major league scout Fred Uhlman: "He's got all the right muscles, but in all the wrong places."

Gonzales wasn't buying the negative stuff—and neither were his employers. The Royals chose Jackson in the fourth round of the amateur free-agent draft in June 1986, and Bo signed a three-year, $1.06 million contract with the American League club within three weeks.

"Everyone had some excuse why they didn't draft Bo," Gonzales said, "but the more I watched him, the more I felt I was watching something that comes along once every 50 years or so."

In Gonzales' scouting report, Bo's potential was rated at 71 on a system in which anything higher than 70 is a superstar. On an individual-category scale that ranks 8.0 as best, Jackson received 8.0 from Gonzales on power, speed and fielding and 7.0 for arm strength.

Another believer was Dick Egan, who was a national cross-checker for the Major League Scouting Bureau. Egan rated Bo's potential at 75.5, the highest overall figure in bureau history.

□

Bo Jackson visited the Kansas City Royals, California Angels and Toronto Blue Jays before the June draft of amateur free-agent talent in 1986. And Bo's agent, Richard Woods, telephoned the Texas Rangers, Baltimore Orioles, San Diego Padres and New York Mets.

Still, John Schuerholz of the Royals and Pat Gillick of the Blue Jays were the only general managers who kept an open mind about the possibility of Jackson choosing baseball over football.

"Skepticism was everywhere," Woods said. "People would wink at us and say, 'C'mon, you guys. What's really the story?' The media, the public, football people, baseball people. Nobody believed us." Nobody except Royals scout Ken Gonzales.

Gonzales was turned on to Jackson when Terry Brasseale, Jackson's baseball coach at McAdory High in McCalla, Ala., telephoned him one day. Gonzales was a onetime graduate assistant coach for Brasseale's team at Montevallo University in Alabama.

"Terry called me about a youngster who was making headlines as a football halfback and breaking records in track and said I ought to see him play baseball," Gonzales said. "That's

The excitement of Bo's single in his first pro at-bat was tempered by his 4-for-45 start as a member of the Chicks.

where it all started with us and Bo. And we spent the next five years scouting his head and his heart."

. Gonzales watched Bo hit 500-foot home runs. He saw him beat out ground balls to second base. And long before Jackson made a one-for-the-book throw at Seattle as a major leaguer, Gonzales saw him unleash a throw considered even better.

"It was against Mississippi State," Gonzales said. "He caught a ball in center field against the fence at the 410-foot sign. The runner went from second to third. Well, Bo threw the ball from the fence to third and split the bag. I mean, it was right there.

"I remember we (scouts) were all just sitting there looking at each other without saying a word. I finally said, 'There's nobody in the big leagues playing today that could make that throw, and here's a 20-year-old kid doing it now.' He's got the best arm in the country. . . He's got such a flair for the dramatic, that I'd love for him to have that opportunity to play in a World Series or Super Bowl. You'd see something special there.

"But to tell you the truth, I don't even follow him in football. I can't watch him. I could just see a linebacker come and clip him from behind and take a couple of knees with him. And I don't want to live with that memory for the rest of my life.

"I don't know if I'll still be alive the next time another Bo Jackson comes around, so I'd just like to enjoy this one as much as I can."

☐

"He needs 600 at-bats, a year and a half (in the minor leagues). He's got to refine all that talent. Right now, he's succeeding on raw ability. He needs to add the little subtleties."
— Larry Himes, then scouting director
for the California Angels, on the baseball future
of Auburn senior Bo Jackson, whose minor league seasoning
actually would last just two months and consist of only 184 at-bats

☐

"I learned something the first day I stepped in the Memphis Chicks' locker room. The thing I had done for fun my whole life was now a job and a responsibility. It was hard to take at first. The more I played, the more I cussed myself for screwing up, the more I realized it's not a hobby, or just something to do. It's a responsibility. . . ."
— Bo Jackson, reflecting on his entry into professional baseball

☐

The 1986 National Football League draft was eight months away and baseball's June sweepstakes was 10 months down the road. Still, specula-

Unfazed by his slow start in the professional ranks, Bo Jackson rebounded to finish his Memphis stint with a .277 average.

tion was heavy about who might be the No. 1-rated player in each talent grab bag.

Incredibly, the same name was coming up—for both drafts, that is.

Vincent Edward (Bo) Jackson.

How good might Auburn's Jackson be as an NFL running back?

"Maybe the best ever," Washington Redskins General Manager Bobby Beathard said. "He's like O.J. (Simpson). Only bigger and stronger. Gosh, it's hard to imagine how much he could do."

His projection as a major league baseball player?

"A No. 3-4-5 hitter with power to hit 40 home runs," said Larry Himes, then director of scouting for the California Angels and now general manager of the Chicago White Sox. Himes quickly added that Jackson also had the capacity to steal 40 bases in a single season.

As it turned out, Bo Jackson was indeed the No. 1 selection in the NFL draft. However, largely because of the belief he would play professional football (and only professional football), Jackson lasted until the fourth round in the baseball pool. His selectors: The Tampa Bay Buccaneers and the Kansas City Royals.

□

Yes, Bo Jackson got a base hit in his first professional at-bat and, yes, he dazzled rivals and spectators alike with his physique and athletic skills. But in his first few weeks with the Memphis Chicks, he didn't overwhelm anyone with his overall baseball ability.

In fact, after rapping a single in his first trip to the plate, Jackson collected only three hits in his next 44 at-bats. A 4-for-45 start in the pro ranks is not exactly the way to get attention—but Bo managed to turn heads even during the tough going.

Exhibit A is the night Jackson was running full tilt for a fly ball. Never letting up in his pursuit, Bo crossed into foul territory and quickly came upon a chain-link fence. What to do?

No problem.

Jackson merely hurdled the four-foot-high barrier and came down squarely on his feet.

Talk about athleticism. Which is exactly what the crowd did, despite the fact Bo didn't come up with the catch.

□

While teammates and rivals alike looked on with fascination and awe as Heisman Trophy-winning Bo Jackson arrived for baseball duty in the Southern League, it didn't take long for opponents to wield the needle once

Bo began to struggle.

Asked if he had struck out the mighty Bo, a pitcher for the Greenville Braves cracked, "Yeah, but who hasn't."

Did Bo's troubling start at Memphis get him down?

"I don't care if I go 2 for 200," Jackson said, "I'm going to have confidence. I'm the type guy that won't let you beat me."

After his second game in a Memphis uniform, Bo Jackson, 1 for 7 at the plate in his young career, had a message for his legion of fans: "Don't expect too much of Bo just because of the name. I have to come into my own whenever the time is right. I'm trying to get there. I just don't want the people out there to build up the hype like I'm a superman."

Bo knew of what he spoke.

Southern League pitchers continued to tug at Superman's cape, and after 45 at-bats Jackson had an embarrassing .089 batting average. How low can you go?

But just as he had told fans not to set their expectations too high, Bo also had promised that—in time—he would deliver. But how could he—or anyone, for that matter—rebound from such a disastrous start? Surely there were some things that even Bo Jackson couldn't do.

This "crisis," though, was not out of Bo's can-do realm. He proceeded to rip Class AA pitching. In mid-July, he went on a week's tear that produced 11 hits in 26 at-bats and included three triples, two homers and eight RBIs. He wound up hitting safely in 40 of his last 48 games with the Chicks, and he batted at a .338 clip—47 hits in 139 at-bats—after the dismal 4-for-45 start.

"He has progressed very, very quickly," Memphis Manager Tommy Jones said during the spurt. "You make a few suggestions here and there, and he'll put them into the game that night."

Bo had indeed "come into his own." With a final .277 average and seven homers for Memphis, Jackson was off to join the big club, the Kansas City Royals.

BASEBALL
IN KANSAS CITY

Not everyone makes his debut in the majors against a pitcher with 321 big-league victories to his credit.

Furthermore, not everyone gets a base hit in his first major league at-bat when going against such an esteemed opponent.

Clearly, not everyone is Bo Jackson.

The date: Tuesday, September 2, 1986. The place: Royals Stadium, Kansas City. The occasion: Royals vs. Chicago White Sox.

A turnout of 17,000-plus was on hand that night as the Hall of Fame-bound pitcher, Steve Carlton, took the mound for the White Sox against a Royals lineup that featured ballyhooed newcomer Jackson, the Heisman Trophy-winning athlete who had just been summoned from Memphis of the Southern League. Bo was listed sixth in the Kansas City batting order and stationed in right field.

Having played a grand total of 53 professional baseball games—all at the Class AA level—before stepping in against one of the game's all-time-great pitchers, Jackson seemed to take the situation in stride. Batting in the second inning, he made his first trip to the plate in the majors a memorable one by legging out an infield hit off the four-time Cy Young Award recipient.

Those familiar with Jackson's ability to meet virtually any challenge hardly were surprised over the way Bo had broken into the big leagues. Of course, those accustomed to Carlton's longtime excellence weren't exactly startled when the 41-year-old lefthander gained the upper hand that evening. Getting ninth-inning relief help from Bobby Thigpen, Carlton wound up a 3-0 winner.

While Bo went hitless in his other two at-bats in the game, he still could reflect on hit No. 1 as a major leaguer. Carlton, meanwhile, could savor victory No. 322.

So Bo Jackson singled off Steve Carlton in his first game in the majors. It wasn't exactly a McCovey-esque beginning.

San Francisco's Willie McCovey, you might recall, broke into the big leagues in 1959 with a 4-for-4 effort—two singles and two triples—against Hall of Famer-to-be Robin Roberts. And since 1900, 10 other players have collected four hits in nine-inning games while making their first appearances in the major leagues.

No, Bo wasn't quite up to a four-hit start. Shoot, it took him until his *fifth* game in the majors to reel off a four-hit performance. Not too shabby, though, considering that no rookie in Royals history had achieved a four-hit game so quickly in his big-league career.

Playing against the Seattle Mariners on the night of September 11,

Steve Carlton, a future Hall of Famer, was pitching for the Chicago White Sox and nearing the end of his career when he gave up a single to Bo Jackson in the youngster's first major league at-bat.

1986, at Royals Stadium, Bo collected four singles—three of which were infield hits—and netted his first major league RBI as Kansas City rebounded from a 6-2 deficit and defeated the Mariners, 7-6, in 10 innings.

□

Bo Jackson's flair for the dramatic was never more evident than on a Sunday afternoon in mid-September of 1986.

It was on that day—September 14, to be exact—that Jackson unloaded his first major league home run. Bo made sure it was no ordinary homer, though. He merely touched off the longest shot in the history of Royals Stadium, a 475-foot blast that landed high on the enbankment beyond the wall in left-center field. His victim was Seattle righthander Mike Moore.

". . . He hits one home run and he's famous!" kidded California's Reggie Jackson two days after Bo Jackson had connected for his mammoth smash off the Mariners' Moore. "They show it on CNN every 20 minutes! He's a superstar already! Around the world in 20 minutes! Let's have a look at him! Tell him to show his face!"

The Kansas City Royals were in Anaheim to open a series against the Angels, and Bo was doing stretching exercises in the clubhouse. Finally, he emerged.

Asked if his first big-league homer had been particularly special, Bo answered, "Yes and no. It was my first one in the majors, but I was concentrating at the time on helping us win the game. Now I look at it as just another hit."

Then came the obligatory "Do you miss football?" query. "No," he responded. "I'm a baseball player."

Bo, whose pregame activities included a chat with Reggie, further showed his face—and his bat—to the Angels' slugger when, with Kansas City trailing by a 5-3 score in the eighth inning, he clubbed a two-run homer off Donnie Moore. The game-tying smash was in vain, though, as California scored once in its half of the eighth and held on for a 6-5 triumph.

Reggie Jackson, an athlete long admired by Bo Jackson, sat out the first two games of the September 16-17-18 Angels-Royals series as the 1986 American League West race entered its final three weeks.

Bo, of course, stole the spotlight in the series opener with a late-game home run that enabled Kansas City to forge a short-lived tie. The Royals' rookie then was a non-factor in game two.

In the series finale, Reggie and Bo played in the same major league game for the first time. And while the kid, Bo, had given Reggie an eyeful

***Bo talks baseball in a 1986 meeting with boyhood hero Reggie Jackson,
who was playing his second to last big-league season with California.***

48 hours earlier, it was now the master's turn.

Reginald Martinez Jackson, 40 years young and a man who had given
baseball some of its greatest theater during his two-decade career, was center stage once more. Reggie pounded three homers and drove in seven runs,
leading the Angels to an 18-3 pasting of the Royals.

□

"I was more happy that Kansas City drafted me in the fourth round than
someone else drafting me in the first round," Bo Jackson said after baseball's June draft of amateur talent in 1986.

"It's really tough to say what would have happened if I was drafted by
another team, like California (which had selected him a year earlier). I'm
not a city boy. I like my privacy. I like to drive, but I hate traffic. I don't
think I'd like to live in a big city."

Bo obviously saw highly desirable qualities in both the Royals' organization and the Kansas City area. The team was the defending World Series
champion and had won two American League pennants and six A.L. West

Division titles in the previous 10 years; plus, the Kansas City metropolitan area was large enough to be "major league" but confined enough to have a small-town feel.

It's not that Bo just couldn't face up to the rigors of life in the big, big city. A little more than a year after signing with the Royals, Jackson decided to play a little more football—for the National Football League's Raiders, who just happened to be headquartered in that apex of traffic and congestion and little privacy, Los Angeles.

□

"What he is, is the best damn free-agent signing in the history of this game."

—San Diego Padres Manager Jack McKeon,
on Bo Jackson, the 105th player selected
in baseball's amateur free-agent draft in June 1986

□

Detroit Manager Sparky Anderson has two distinct—and widely differing—recollections that speak volumes about the breadth of Bo Jackson's baseball skills. One involves a monstrous home run; the other a mere ground ball.

"In Fort Myers (in 1987)," said Anderson, referring to Kansas City's former Florida spring-training base, "he hit a ball up over that scoreboard out there in center. We were trying to determine just what the distance would be—between 550 and 600 feet. It was off Bill Laskey, a hanging slider.

"Billy Muffett (Tigers pitching coach) to this day talks about it. I mean, you cannot hit a ball farther or harder."

Power.

The grounder also came in a Tigers-Royals game, this time on the artificial turf at Royals Stadium. Jackson "hit a two-bouncer to short," Anderson recounted. "The ball was fielded clean by (Alan) Trammell and thrown, and he was safe. It was like, 'How could that be?'"

Speed.

Anderson can scarcely believe that one man could be so strong and so fast.

"He also broke a bat on us and hit one to right-center (in Royals Stadium), where the waterfall is," Sparky added. "It didn't go in the waterfall, but it was below the waterfall and the bat was broke."

The Tigers' manager is profuse in his praise of Jackson on other fronts, too, but he acknowledges reservations about Bo's desire to play both major

By 1988, young left fielder Bo Jackson combined the blazing speed of Kansas City center fielder Willie Wilson (center) and the power of right fielder Danny Tartabull (right) into one impressive package.

league baseball and professional football.

"I said when he came (to the majors) if everybody just left him alone and let him play, in due time, there's no telling what he'll do," Anderson said. "I certainly think he's the greatest athlete in the game as far as sheer athletic ability. I can't imagine anybody could do more than he can do.

"The thing that impresses me so much about him now is his defense. His defense is so much improved over when he first started. He was coming in on balls, and they'd be over his head. He'd go back on balls and had to come forward.

"I would like to see him still finish football . . . and just get with the baseball. Because then I think you'd really see (something). Because he has to have some time; you can't just go from one to the other. Mentally, it's too hard. They can talk all they want about the physical part. You can be so strong that you can do things. But you need a mental rest, too.

"You cannot concentrate the way you have to concentrate. You've been having to do that in one sport, which is totally different, and then switch over and do it in another one . . . He's done it, but I think if he continues to do it, you're going to see a backtrack in one of the two places."

□

It was 1988 at Arlington Stadium and Bo Jackson was eyeing a table set up for card-playing in the visiting-team clubhouse.

Royals teammate Willie Wilson was walking by when Jackson said, "Hey, you think I can jump on it?"

"What are you talking about?" Wilson wondered.

"The table, you think I can jump on the table?" Bo responded.

Wilson: "You're crazy, man. What do you want to do something stupid like that for?"

Jackson: "I just want to see if I can do it, that's all."

Wilson: "What, with a running start?"

Jackson: "Nah, just standing there."

Wilson: "No way, man, no way."

Jackson took one last, so-you-don't-believe-me look at Wilson, strolled toward the table, bent into a crouch and leaped.

Wilson could only laugh when, in the next second, he saw Jackson standing atop the table, arms raised as if he had just climbed Mount Everest.

"That's the thing about Bo," Wilson said. "You know, I wonder if there's anything that dude can't do."

□

Bob Boone, who has caught more games than any catcher in big-league history, is a physical-fitness fanatic. In the off-season, he works out a couple hours in the morning, three hours in the afternoon and then rides a bicycle for enjoyment at night.

"I've always been dedicated to my workouts," Boone said. "If I wasn't, I know there's no way I'd still be in this game."

Forget the fact that Boone is 42 years old. He boasts rippling biceps, wide shoulders and a flat stomach. Fact is, in his years with the California Angels (1982 through 1988), Boone thought his physique was second to none among players on the American League club.

Then Bob Boone joined the Kansas City Royals and got a look at a bare-chested Bo Jackson.

"I couldn't believe it," Boone said. "Never in my life have I seen a body like that.

"So I go up to Bo and ask him how he keeps a body like that. I figure he's going to go into this big weight-lifting spiel, and everything else, and you know what he tells me? 'Nothing.'

"He says he doesn't do anything to keep that body. Finally, he tells me he'll do some pushups and situps, but that's it.

"You know, every time I work out now, I think about that body. Some folks are more fortunate than others. . . ."

□

On the road, the Royals go through their pregame stretching in the clubhouse. At home, however, they filter onto the Royals Stadium turf before batting practice to do their exercises. It's a relaxed time, with the players bantering at the start of their workday.

Bo Jackson tends to enliven the late-afternoon ritual.

"Every time we go out to stretch, we go sit behind the batting cage," Royals pitcher Bret Saberhagen said. "He'll sit on his butt and without coming up, he'll throw a ball on a line and hit the press-box window and make the reporter sitting there jump. I

Kansas City catcher Bob Boone, a physical-fitness fanatic, was amazed the first time he got a look at Bo's physique.

know I couldn't get it halfway up there, let alone be that accurate. His arm just really amazes me."

□

The setting was Florida and the event was a launch.

No, the blastoff didn't occur at Cape Canaveral. Instead, the scene was the Kansas City Royals' spring-training park in Baseball City.

Furthermore, this was an unscheduled launch—just ask pitcher Dennis (Oil Can) Boyd.

Boyd was toiling for the Boston Red Sox in a March 5, 1989, exhibition game against the Royals when Bo Jackson got all of one of his pitches. *All* of it.

The ball soared toward center field and kept climbing—right over the 71-foot-high scoreboard. Unquestionably, some space shots are more wondrous than others, and this one left onlookers agape as they stared off into the wild blue yonder.

"Somebody asked me what he hit," Royals first-base coach Bob Schaefer said. "I said it was a Top-Flite."

Royals Manager John Wathan, who hit 21 home runs in a 10-season career in the major leagues, was taken aback by Bo's mighty clout, which traveled an estimated 515 feet.

"You don't know if you'll see one hit that far the rest of your life," Wathan said. "How often do you see a ball hit 500 feet? I don't care if it's spring training. I don't care if the wind's blowing. That's the farthest one I've ever seen. I'm thinking, 'It's going to hit the scoreboard' . . . then it carried over. Unbelievable."

Wathan was asked whether Jackson's smash reminded him of any of his big-league homers. "About five . . . put together," he cracked.

Kansas City pitcher Bret Saberhagen was suitably impressed, but the righthander couldn't resist a gibe.

"He still owes me $100," Saberhagen said. "He told me he's going to hit one off the Royals Stadium scoreboard and he hasn't done that yet. I think if he wanted to bad enough, he probably could."

Royals coach John Mayberry, a man who packed considerable wallop during his playing days (he once hit 34 homers in one season for Kansas City), also said the blow was the longest he had ever witnessed.

"If I see Reggie Jackson," Mayberry said, "I'm going to tell him, 'This man makes your home runs look like popups.' "

Andrew Hoppen, a parking attendant at the Baseball City complex, thought he was seeing things. Suddenly, out of the blue, it came. A baseball. From where, Hoppen wasn't quite sure.

After all, he was parking cars well beyond the confines of the stadium. But there it was, a white missile, rising above the massive scoreboard and then dropping just inside a wide fence near the parking lot.

Hoppen had a one-word reaction to what he had just seen: "Wow!"

Typically, Bo Jackson wasn't quite as impressed. He couldn't understand all the hoopla over a spring-training feat.

Kansas City coach John Mayberry, a former Royals first baseman who packed considerable wallop during his playing days, was quickly impressed by the magnitude of Bo's powerful blasts.

Grudgingly, Bo finally talked about the homer—and even acknowledged a smidgen of satisfaction.

"It doesn't mean that much," he said, "but it's nice to see it travel like that."

Pat Williams, general manager of the National Basketball Association's Orlando Magic, has seen some pretty remarkable things in his long career as a sports executive.

An NBA general manager for most of the last 20 years and a former award-winning executive in minor league baseball, Williams, a frequent visitor to Royals exhibition games, was asked to name the most extraordinary accomplishment he had ever seen in any sport.

Remember now, this is a man who ran the Philadelphia 76ers in the days when Julius Erving was performing the unfathomable for the NBA club. Williams also has watched Michael Jordan defy the laws of gravity, and he has seen the likes of Jerry West, Wilt Chamberlain, Kareem Abdul-Jabbar, Walt Frazier, Larry Bird and Magic Johnson work their magic.

"It's got to be that homer Bo hit off Oil Can Boyd, you know, the one that cleared the scoreboard," said Williams, a Philadelphia native, as he zeroed in on the No. 1 feat. "It was one of those home runs you see once in a lifetime. It reminded me of balls Dick Allen used to hit over the Alpo sign (in deep left-center field) at Connie Mack Stadium in Philadelphia."

Toronto Blue Jays scout Gordon Lakey may be a little vague on the details—"I don't even remember who Kansas City was playing or who the pitcher was"—but a ball that Bo Jackson hit at Royals Stadium in 1989 otherwise made quite an impression on him.

"Bo was at the plate and he hit a home run to right field, well, I guess it was right field," Lakey explained. "I kept looking for the ball, but I never saw it. I mean, I never saw the thing land. The thing just disappeared.

"The only thing I can figure is that he knocked the air out of the ball."

□

Of the 32 home runs that Bo hit for Kansas City in 1989, the very first may have set the tone for Jackson's breakthrough season as a major leaguer.

Homer No. 1 came at Royals Stadium on April 8 against Boston Red Sox ace Roger Clemens. It was a blustery, 44-degree afternoon—in other words, the conditions were not exactly ideal for trying to get around on the offerings of one of the game's hardest throwers.

Jackson struck out in his first two trips to the plate in that Saturday game, making him 0 for 13 with nine strikeouts in head-to-head duels with Clemens since the start of the 1988 season. However, the second of those strikeouts in their early-'89 meeting was a gritty encounter—one that Royals star George Brett reflects on with considerable admiration.

"He fouled off some curveballs," Brett said. "He fouled off some split-fingers. He fouled off high fastballs, which are tough to do on Clemens, and he just kept fouling them off.

"You could tell he was getting tired up there, and you could tell Clemens was getting tired of throwing them in. Finally, he slipped one by him, and Bo came back and said, 'Man, he just wore me down. I was too tired to swing. But I'll get him the next time.'"

Prophetic words.

On his next at-bat, in the seventh inning, Jackson unloaded on Clemens. He drove a 1-1 fastball over the wall in right-center, tying the score at 1-1. The Royals went on to win, 2-1, in 10 innings and Bo went on to a enjoy a big season that included 105 RBIs.

□

"I hit it off the end of my bat," said Bo Jackson, referring to the landmark blow he had just struck at the Metrodome in Minneapolis.

There was no indication that the Royals' left fielder was kidding, either.

It was May 16, 1989, and Bo had just become the first righthanded batter to hammer a ball into the upper deck of the Metrodome's right-field sector. He connected for the home run against Minnesota Twins righthander Francisco Oliveras, who was making his first major league start.

"Really, it was just another hit as far as I was concerned," Jackson said of the 404-foot drive.

As distant as many of Bo's home runs are, power isn't always the focal point when the discussion centers on Jackson. In the same game in which he slammed the homer high and deep to right off Oliveras, Jackson also stole home.

"I think his speed is probably the thing that really gets your attention," Twins Manager Tom Kelly said. "You try to watch the ball when the ball's hit in the gap, but when he's on first, well, hell, I try to watch him. There aren't many guys you watch running the bases. You're always watching the ball go into the gap or down the line. You watch the ball and you watch the fielder get the ball. That's one guy (Bo), I watch him run. It's quite entertaining, even if he is on the other team.

"The thing we always said was that if he improved 100 percent, he's going to be a pretty good player. And he's certainly done that. I hate to think that he's going to improve a little more, but I imagine he will."

When Bo hit a prodigious lefthanded home run during batting practice at the Metrodome in Minneapolis, it was almost more than Twins star Kirby Puckett could comprehend.

The night before poling that homer into the right-field upper deck at the Metrodome, Bo had one swing left in batting practice at the Twins' ballpark.

Having had what he considered enough conventional batting practice, Jackson jumped into the cage and dug in from the left side of the plate. He took a hack—and the ball soared over the plastic fence in right, past the dome lights and crashed off a sign on the facade of the second deck in right-center field, some 450 feet away, about 30 feet shy of the longest ball ever hit at the Metrodome.

Bo laughed, shrugged his shoulders at astonished onlookers, grabbed his glove and headed to the outfield.

"That's the damnedest thing I've ever seen," Twins center fielder Kirby Puckett said. "Can you believe that? I've never hit a ball that far to that part of the dome in my life. And this guy does it lefthanded. Give me a break."

□

Things haven't always been rosy for Bo Jackson in Kansas City. For proof positive, consider the mood in the summer of 1987 when Bo announced he was going to play pro football as well as major league baseball.

If Bo had any questions about the way Royals fans would treat him after his disclosure that he'd be spending his autumn months playing for the National Football League's Los Angeles Raiders, well, the answers weren't long in coming.

Taking the field at Royals Stadium for the first time after announcing

Frank White, pictured greeting Bo Jackson after a 1987 home run, was one of the Royals veterans critical of the youngster after his announcement that he would play pro football during the off-season.

that he would tackle football in his spare time, Jackson found himself a target—literally—of fans' criticism at the July 16 Royals-Orioles game. Plastic footballs, rubber footballs, even leather footballs, came raining down on him. It was the demonstrative fans' way of telling Jackson just what they thought of his renewed enthusiasm for football—an interest that in their view might detract from his baseball performance and possibly even lead to the end of his diamond career.

Royals players also were upset—furious might be a better word—that team management was acceding to Bo's wish to play football. Here was Jackson, the new guy on the block, getting a stunning go-ahead on a remarkable request when veteran players seemingly had to fight for any special favors.

"It's like Bo is bigger than the Royals," center fielder Willie Wilson said in July 1987. "...We've got guys playing here for years, then they let a three-month player come in here and tell them what to do. I'm so mad I can't stand it."

"The game's not about winning anymore," second baseman Frank White said. "It's about putting a show on the field. . . ."

The uproar over Bo took its toll on team unity and on Jackson himself. The Royals wound up only two games out of first place at season's end in the '87 American League West race, but the ball club lacked its usual cohesiveness in the stretch run. The hubbub's effect on Bo? He struggled so much in the second half of the '87 season—he had belted 18 homers and driven in 45 runs by the All-Star break—that he finished the year on the bench. He hit just .188 after the break with four homers and eight RBIs.

Bo Jackson survived the unpleasantness of 1987 by winning the respect of his Royals teammates. Perhaps most important, he *earned* that respect.

Bo arrived six days early for spring training in 1988, worked out in the batting cage before his teammates would arrive at the ballpark and sneaked away at lunch time to take fly balls.

"If he had come here and didn't work hard, and we saw a lot of preferential treatment," Frank White said, "I think we would have said, 'What's going on here?' But when he gave 100 percent like he did, what could any of us say?

"You've got to remember, Bo had to make adjustments, too. Bo was a superstar coming in. Everybody in the United States knew who Bo Jackson was. Guys aren't used to seeing rookies walk in here and holding press conferences every day.

"And when Bo was allowed to do something that the rest of us weren't allowed to do in their contract, that made guys feel a little different."

George Brett winces when he recalls the summer of '87.

"The fans of Kansas City turned their backs on him and made life absolutely miserable for him," the Royals' standout said. "They were trying to destroy a young man with all the athletic ability in the world. And they knew it was working. It got to a point where he couldn't do anything. When he started misplaying routine fly balls, it was evident that they were getting to him."

"We betrayed him," Willie Wilson said of Bo's teammates. "At a time he needed us the most, we abandoned him. We didn't care how he played or care what happened to him. Instead, we blamed him for all our problems. He didn't need that abuse, especially from his teammates."

As history has shown, Jackson proved he could play both sports quite nicely—and his dedication to baseball and the Royals now goes virtually unchallenged. After all, it's the football season—not the baseball schedule —that Bo curtails.

Two-sport man Bo Jackson prepares to loft a pass to pitcher Mark Gubicza (right) as teammates Danny Jackson (second from left) and George Brett look on prior to a 1987 game at Royals Stadium.

In 1988, with the unrest behind him, Bo began to blossom as a big-league baseball player. He cracked 25 home runs for the Royals, stole 27 bases and made tremendous strides defensively. Then, in 1989, he put up big-time numbers: 32 home runs, 105 RBIs, 86 runs scored and a .495 slugging percentage.

Does Jackson look back with anguish at the fuss of '87? Does he harbor ill feeling toward fans and teammates?

"I don't even think about the past," he said. "You can't go far in life if you dwell in the past. I'm going to keep working hard and try to entertain them (the fans). That's all I've ever tried to do."

□

It was the fifth inning of a May 23, 1989, game at Arlington, Tex., and the Kansas City Royals were playing the Texas Rangers. Bo Jackson was at the plate against Rangers fireballer Nolan Ryan, who at that juncture had faced Bo six times in the major leagues and struck him out on each occasion.

Ryan's first pitch brushed back Jackson and his second offering sent

Two of Bo's most memorable home runs were hit against two of baseball's top pitchers: Texas' Nolan Ryan (left) and Boston's Roger Clemens.

the Royals' outfielder sprawling.

Not particularly pleased that a ball had just whistled past his head, Jackson got up slowly and stared—or maybe even glared—at Ryan. He took a vicious cut at Ryan's next pitch and missed.

By now, the crowd was very much into the Ryan-Jackson battle and it watched with anticipation as Bo popped his bubble gum and dug his cleats into the ground. On the next pitch, Jackson made contact. And how. The ball took off like a shot and landed halfway up the bleachers in center field.

The home run drive was measured at 461 feet, the longest blow in

Arlington Stadium's 18-year history as a major league ballpark. To many observers, the distance seemed much greater than that.

"The guy upstairs needs to get a new tape measure," cracked Jackson, who then startled the assembled media with this disclosure: "Really, I was just trying to put the ball in play."

The night was noteworthy beyond Bo's prodigious home run. It marked the first time Jackson had batted cleanup in the major leagues.

"I'm not one to get all hyped up about moving up in the lineup," Jackson said before the game. "I'm here to play baseball, whether they put me first, fourth, sixth or ninth in the lineup."

Jackson's homer, a three-run shot, seemed to inspire the Royals. Down by a 10-0 score after four innings, Kansas City closed within 10-8 by game's end.

Was the Texas club trying to send a message to Bo Jackson with the tight pitches?

"I don't think fear is one of the things you have to worry about with Bo," Rangers Manager Bobby Valentine said. "I don't think he has fear. He doesn't know the word. As far as intimidation, you don't intimidate an intimidator."

Considering that Jackson had entered the 1989 season with fewer than 1,000 at-bats in the big leagues, Valentine said he was "amazed" at the adjustments Jackson had been able to make. "That takes outstanding athletic ability," Valentine said, "and he has the most athletic ability, I think, of anybody I've ever seen play baseball."

□

First impressions can be deceiving—or at least confusing—and such was the case when one baseball man got his initial look at the talents of one Bo Jackson.

Even when a prospect's negative points seem to offset the positive, a scout—such as Toronto's Gordon Lakey—can see a ray of hope in the aspiring ballplayer. Jackson, for instance, presented a curious mix when he surfaced in the major leagues in September 1986.

On the down side, Bo played the outfield with Lonnie Smith-like finesse; plus, at the plate, he wrapped his bat behind his head in a way that limited his chances of making hard contact. In the good-news department, Jackson possessed impressive bat speed, to be sure, and he certainly could run. Maybe the varied package was to be expected, considering that Bo's professional experience amounted to only 184 at-bats for Class AA Memphis.

What to make of this guy?

Lakey, who scouts the American League as an advance man for the Blue Jays, wasn't overwhelmed with what he saw of a raw Jackson in 1986 and 1987 and, to some extent, even as recently as 1988. What he was witness to in 1989 was a different story.

"At first I thought he was a football player who plays baseball," Lakey said. "Now I look at him as a baseball player who plays football. In my own perception, that's the biggest change.

"Not many players in the league can beat you five ways. He can beat you with his speed. He can beat you with his power. He can beat you with his bat. He can beat you in the field. He can beat you with his arm. Ellis Burks (Boston) can do it. Devon White (California) can do it. Ruben Sierra (Texas) can do it. But there's not a whole lot of them."

☐

"Nothing surprises me anymore what that guy can do. He can run like hell, and he can hit the ball out of Yellowstone Park. What more do you want? You've got to go back to Mays and Mantle to find anyone with that kind of combination."

—scout Hugh Alexander, discussing Bo Jackson's
banner 1989 season with the Royals

☐

Harold Reynolds sat alone in the Seattle Mariners' clubhouse, his eyes transfixed on the videotape machine. He moved his hand back and forth. Whir. Fast-forward. Whir. Fast-rewind. Whir.

Reynolds could not take his eyes off the videotape. The more times he saw the 10-second footage, the more bewildered he was. But if he hadn't taken time to view the tape, he never would have believed what had transpired earlier that evening.

How could a man, standing flat-footed, throw a baseball 300 feet, fire a perfect strike and nail the Mariners' fastest runner as if he were standing still?

"It's crazy," Reynolds said. "I was there. I was the one thrown out. I've got it on replay. And I still don't believe it. I'm telling you right now, the guy is superhuman."

What the fuss was all about on the night of June 5, 1989, at Seattle's Kingdome can be summed up in two words: The Throw. Clearly, the remarkable play will live forever in Kansas City Royals baseball lore.

And just who let fly with the ball from his station in left field? Why,

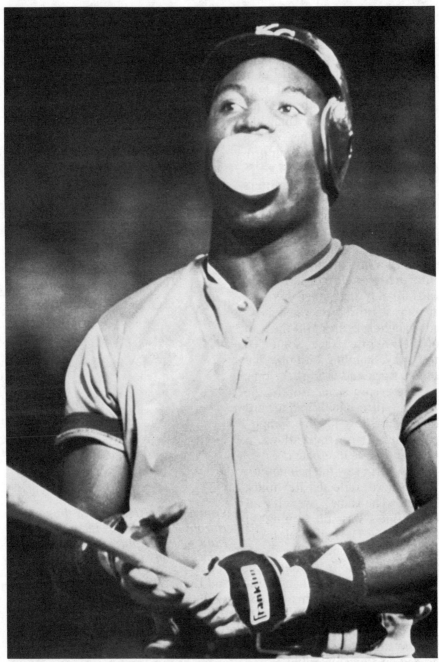

Bo was the picture of relaxation as he prepared to face Nolan Ryan in a 1989 confrontation that would result in a memorable 461-foot homer.

none other than Vincent Edward
(Bo) Jackson.

"It is the greatest throw I've
ever seen in my life," Royals Manager John Wathan said. "If I'm in
the game another 30 years, I don't
think I'll ever see another like it."

"I've never seen anything like
it," emphasized Mariners coach
Bob Didier, who has been in professional baseball since 1967.

The Royals and Mariners
were deadlocked, 3-3, in the 10th
inning when the play unfolded:
With Reynolds at first base, and
running on the pitch, Scott Bradley lined a fastball off Steve Farr
into the left-field corner. Reynolds already had taken his first
steps past third base when Jackson caught the carom off the wall
at the warning track, some 300
feet away. Standing with one foot
on the track and lacking the time
to take even a stride toward the
plate, Bo turned and fired toward
home. Just how much "oomph"
could he get on the ball when
throwing while flat-footed?

"When I saw the ball go into
the corner," reflected Reynolds,
"I said, 'The game's over. It's all
over.' But I was still coming on
hard. I saw Darnell (Coles, the
on-deck hitter) put his hands up
so I could come in standing up,

*Speedy Seattle second baseman
Harold Reynolds was Bo's victim in a
June 5, 1989, play that came to be
known simply as "The Throw."*

but then he throws his hands down, and I say, 'What?'

"So I'm about to throw a courtesy slide, and I see the ball in (catcher)
Bob Boone's mitt. I say, 'You've got to be kidding me.'"

Boone, who had been standing at ease trying to make Reynolds believe
that no throw was coming, was forced to give up his charade as the ball
headed on a line toward him.

"When it was hit, I felt our only chance was to decoy him and hope he slows up," Boone said. "Then I'm looking at the throw, and I say, 'This ball's carrying all the way to me.'

"I can't believe it. So, I forget about the deke so I can catch the ball and tag him out.

"It's still amazing to me. Not many people in the world can throw the ball that far, but I don't know anybody who can just grab it and throw it as far and accurate as he did. The man is incredible."

The play so fooled the umpiring crew that when Jackson's throw got to Boone, home-plate umpire Larry Young was down the third-base line and Jim Joyce was still at first base. There was no one around to make the call. That's where Farr stepped in.

"You know, not many people realized it, but I wasn't even thinking about backing up the plate," Farr said. "I thought we had no play at all. I wasn't even watching the play because I thought the game was over.

"Then the ball just came out of nowhere. I saw there were no umpires there, so I just made the 'out' sign, you know, to help them out."

After several seconds of delay, Young made the call from about 45 feet away.

"Out!"

"The thing that got me," Wathan said, "was that it was a strike. It was a pitch not too many hitters could even hit because it was on the outside corner. And to think pitchers have trouble from 60 feet, six inches."

When Reynolds retreated to the Mariners' dugout, questioning his own speed, a teammate informed him that Jackson's throw was in the air all the way.

"I said, 'No way. Get out of here,'" Reynolds said. "Then I asked someone else. . . ."

Bradley, who had watched Jackson propel a batting-practice pitch 450 feet into the upper deck in center field, said: "Now, I've seen it all. I mean, is there anything the guy can't do? Really, what can't he do?"

Mariners Manager Jim Lefebvre said: "He's such a tremendous talent. God, I don't know why he even considers football. That was just a supernatural, unbelievable play. He's an incredible specimen."

Jackson, who merely shrugged when teammates kept asking him how he managed to make the throw, almost seemed embarrassed over the commotion.

"I just caught the ball off the wall, turned and threw. End of story," Jackson said. "It's nothing to brag about. Don't try to make a big issue out of it. It's just another throw."

Right, and the Mona Lisa was just another painting by Leonardo da Vinci.

"I take pride in my defense," Jackson said when pressed to talk about the throw. "I think I'm a better defensive player than offensive player. I'm not impressed how far I can hit the ball, but like I said, I do take pride in my defense."

The Royals' George Brett, a two-time American League batting champion and a 13-time All-Star Game selection, sat back and took it all in, uttering not one word. He couldn't get his mind off the throw. And this was a man who had accomplished some truly remarkable feats in his career.

Finally, Brett spoke.

"This is not a normal guy," Brett said. "This guy's a super human being. You don't ever want to quit watching one of our games because you might miss something he does.

"Every series, he does one thing that's going to open your eyes. You just stand there and say, 'Wow.' And that's what I did tonight."

Teammate Bill Buckner put it succinctly: "Just another chapter in the Bo Jackson legend, huh?"

OK, so Bo's heroics saved Kansas City from defeat in the bottom of the 10th inning. Did the Royals, in fact, take advantage of their good fortune and beat the Mariners that night?

Indeed they did.

The score remained 3-3 through the 12th, then the Royals scored two 13th-inning runs off Seattle relief pitchers Tom Niedenfuer and Steve Trout and notched a 5-3 victory.

For Jackson, a scene-stealing act in the Kingdome was nothing new. A little more than a year and a half earlier, while wearing another uniform, he had dazzled Seattle fans with his legs, not his arm.

Wearing the silver and black of the Los Angeles Raiders instead of the blue and white of the Kansas City Royals, Bo had reeled off a 91-yard touchdown run and rushed for 221 yards overall in a National Football League game against the Seattle Seahawks.

□

"There were butterflies when I was in the on-deck circle, but once you get into the batter's box, there's no time to think. You just put your tunnel vision on the pitcher and do what comes naturally."

—Bo Jackson, reflecting on his thoughts
of July 11, 1989, as he awaited his first-ever
at-bat in All-Star Game competition

What comes naturally for Bo Jackson comes rarely, if at all, for many athletes. And that first All-Star at-bat, perhaps more than any of his amateur and pro sports achievements, epitomized Bo's knack of elevating his game to another level.

Jackson, the focus of mounting acclaim because of his two-sport prowess with the Los Angeles Raiders and the Kansas City Royals, was still a bit of a baseball curiosity when he stepped to the plate to face San Francisco's Rick Reuschel in the first inning of the 1989 All-Star Game at Anaheim Stadium. Sure, Bo had compiled impressive statistics in the first three months of the season—he had 21 home runs and 59 RBIs at the All-Star break—and he had been voted a starter for the American League All-Stars. But there were those who needed just a bit more convincing that Bo Jackson already had earned a place among baseball's elite.

With both doubters and believers looking on, leadoff hitter Jackson strode to the plate for the first time in a baseball showcase event. After taking Reuschel's first pitch for a ball, Bo took the righthander's second offering for a ride. As if shot out of a cannon, the ball rocketed toward center field.

Reuschel, in an uncharacteristic move for the veteran pitcher, turned around to watch. The ball remained in flight an agonizingly long time for Reuschel, finally landing on a tarpaulin beyond the center-field fence, 448 feet from home plate.

Jaws dropped, from Anaheim to Altoona.

Bo was just getting started, though. After the show of brute force, he exhibited amazing speed in his next at-bat by beating out a routine double-play relay (a play on which he netted his second RBI of the night) and then stealing second base. Later, he rifled a single to center.

A folk hero—and All-Star Game MVP—had been born.

"He's got something extra," American League Manager Tony La Russa said of Bo Jackson. "He's in a league somewhere up in the heavens."

Among those sharing La Russa's sentiments after the A.L.'s 5-3 triumph were the 64,000-plus fans at Anaheim Stadium, a national television audience, the media, Bo's teammates and Bo's opponents.

Especially the opponents.

"I thought I made a good pitch," Rick Reuschel said of the home run ball. "He just went down and got it. I heard about his power and strength, and I saw it firsthand tonight."

St. Louis' Ozzie Smith, a noted wizard of ah's in his own right, could hardly contain himself.

"How many ways can you say he's great?" Smith asked. "The people got to see what they came to see."

National League Manager Tom Lasorda said Jackson "is an exciting player—he's awesome." Lasorda also remarked that Bo's long-distance home run "sounded like a golf shot."

San Francisco's Will Clark, one of the game's rising stars and a player not particularly modest about his own talents, said someone of Bo's capabilities comes along "once in a decade, if you're lucky."

Tony Gwynn, on the way to his fourth N.L. batting title, was another observer who couldn't quite grasp what he had just seen.

"Bo can do anything," San Diego's Gwynn said. "He changes the way people think of the game. He's redefining the game as we speak. . . ."

□

"He's not just power and speed, he's a competitor."
—Oakland Athletics Manager Tony La Russa,
commenting on the intense enthusiasm exhibited
by Bo Jackson in the 1989 All-Star Game

"I don't think I've seen anybody combine power and speed like that since Mickey Mantle."
—Los Angeles Dodgers Manager Tom Lasorda,
after getting a look at Bo Jackson and his MVP
performance in the '89 All-Star Game

"You're my new idol."
—Minnesota's Kirby Puckett, in a tip-of-the-hat
remark to Bo Jackson after Bo had slammed
his monstrous All-Star Game homer

"I think it will make for a lot of excitement right away."
—Prophetic Tony La Russa, explaining the American
League brain trust's decision to place
power-hitting Bo Jackson at the top of the
batting order for the 1989 All-Star Game

"I don't think about history, but this may be special when I can sit down and tell the story to my grandkids. . . ."
—Bo Jackson, pondering his
Most Valuable Player performance
in his first All-Star Game

"As soon as I saw him hit that first-inning home run, I knew this was

Bo proudly displays the MVP trophy that he earned with his performance in baseball's 1989 All-Star Game.

going to be an amazing night. It's like the moon and stars had to be in some kind of special alignment."
> —Nike advertising director Scott Bedbury, on
> the fact his company introduced a new Bo Jackson
> spot during the All-Star Game telecast

☐

"I'd seen him on commercials on ESPN, and that was enough."

Minnesota righthander Rick Aguilera was discussing the menacing presence of one Bo Jackson, left fielder for the Kansas City Royals. It was September 9, 1989, and Aguilera had just seen Jackson firsthand at Royals Stadium. Bo had doubled twice and driven in all of the Royals' runs in Kansas City's 3-1 victory over Aguilera and the Twins.

Jackson's first double went whizzing in the direction of Twins center fielder Kirby Puckett and rocketed off the wall near the 410-foot sign.

"I didn't even see it until it hit the wall," Puckett said. "It was a bullet. I'm just amazed at the guy. Every year he keeps getting better and better. It's scary to think if he concentrated on baseball what he could do."

Twins Manager Tom Kelly was shaking his head, too.

"The ball that he hit to the 410 sign, right at the bottom of the fence, he hit that ball up here," said Kelly, holding his arms close to his shoulders. "He didn't even get his arms out, and it went 410 feet. . . ."

☐

"All he can do is go up, knock you down and dunk."
> —Devon White's way of saying that while
> Bo Jackson's strength is evident in any endeavor,
> his varied athletic talents do not
> extend to at least one sport, basketball
> (White, of the California Angels, once
> went against Bo in a multi-sport competition.)

☐

"Baseball was fun when I was in college. It's my job now. But I like my 3-to-11 shift."
> —Bo Jackson, comparing major
> league baseball to the game
> he played at Auburn

Bo Jackson's privacy is sacred. Just ask the strangers who are greeted with an icy glare when they invade his space in public.

Beneath that intimidating exterior, however, is a big-hearted but publicity-shy samaritan who has performed enough good deeds to give a Boy Scout a guilt trip.

There was the time back in college when Jackson was driving to his summer job at a Birmingham, Ala., bank. A woman lost control of her car, slammed into a guardrail and lay dazed inside the smoking vehicle. Bo rushed to the woman's aid, dragging her to safety moments before the car caught afire. His job done, he slipped off to work as police and paramedics restored order.

"You know, he never even told me a word about it," said Bo's wife, Linda. "I didn't know about it until I read it in the papers."

Mum was also the word when Jackson was relaxing in his Los Angeles condominium, watching a junior college basketball game on TV. The announcer made note of one particular player who had been hampered by his inability to find new shoes big enough to fit his size 21 feet.

Bo picked up the telephone, spoke with his representatives at Nike and had a pair of specially made shoes shipped to the player. There was a catch, however. Bo instructed Nike and the school not to breathe a word to anyone.

Jackson was out shopping for shoes himself in February 1989 when he happened upon two accident victims sitting inside their car on a Kansas City highway. Bo veered to the side of the road, rushed to a house to call an ambulance, then waited with the couple until help arrived.

"There were eight or nine people who slowed down," Jackson said, "but they went right past them. I couldn't believe it. Even if it was my worst enemy, I'd stop and help."

□

OK, so Bo pulls down an annual income that dwarfs what the average Joe makes in a lifetime. Why try to relate? Jackson doesn't flash it in anyone's face. "I came from nothing," he says, "so I can be comfortable with nothing."

You see, Jackson's quest goes beyond the almighty dollar. Listen up:

"If I'm going to go broke, I'm going to go broke taking care of my family.

"My first winter after joining the Royals, I bought three vehicles. I bought my little brother a used Cutlass. For Christmas, I wanted to do something nice for my aunt, so I bought her a new Cadillac. And my mom, I bought her a new van.

"We've lived in the same house since I was in the second grade, so I also wanted to get my mom a new home. But she refuses to move. So I redecorated my mom's kitchen and had everything new put in.

"Oh yeah, and for whoever wants to go to college, I set up college funds for my 26 nieces and nephews."

□

Royals center fielder Willie Wilson was leaving Milwaukee County Stadium with his soon-to-be wife, Catherine. Just outside the ball park, they confronted a mean group that began taunting Wilson with racial insults.

Words were exchanged. Threats were made. Jackson sat in the team bus, watching the nasty scene unfold outside his window.

Bo stepped outside. Eyes widened. The group backed off.

"Everyone had their sleeves rolled up, ready to go," Wilson said, "and that's when they caught a glimpse of Bo."

End of incident.

"Bo's that kind of person," Wilson said. "He doesn't like to be the center of attention, but when it comes down to helping people, he's soft-hearted. People don't realize what a good person he is, but he's one of the finest persons I've ever known."

□

Bo knows bows.

Ask any number of teammates who have followed him underneath the stands at Royals Stadium. A side quiver of arrows and bow in hand, Jackson holds them spellbound as he shoots arrow after arrow into the black of a makeshift target.

"Bo is awesome with a bow," said Royals infielder Kurt Stillwell, who should know. Stillwell joined Jackson at Lake Pewaukee in Wisconsin when Bo added a new sport to his outdoor portfolio: carp fishing . . . with a bow.

"He got three and I got a half—he wounded it and then I got it," Stillwell said.

Since his first hunting trip during his college days at Auburn, Jackson has become an avid outdoorsman. He is a member of Buckmasters, the largest organization of deer hunters in the nation, and has made the switch to archery hunter after years of hunting deer with a rifle.

Speaking to a group of bow hunters from Missouri, Jackson described his first kill with a bow.

"You know the old saying that you have to be completely camouflaged to get a deer with a bow?" he related. "Well, that's not true. I went out

*Deerslayer Bo Jackson, who bagged a 12-point buck in the January 1989
Buckmasters One-Shot Hunt in Alabama.*

*By the end of the 1989 season, Bo's bat-breaking-over-the-thigh routine
was becoming old hat around the American League.*

there in my white Nikes and I stuck out. But I went out there at quarter to four in the afternoon and half an hour later I had my buck."

In January 1989, Bo was participating in his first Buckmasters One-Shot Hunt, a competiton in which celebrities are guided by local deer hunters and limited to one shot with a rifle.

"Bo got up in a treestand and he spotted a deer," said Jackie Bushman, founder of Buckmasters. "When it started to walk away, Bo whistled real loud, the deer froze and Bo shot it."

It was a 12-point buck, the largest felled in the hunt.

□

When Bo Jackson saunters into the cage for batting practice, all activity ceases. Concession lines empty. Teammates and opponents alike stop to stare, transfixed by the swing that propels mammoth blasts to points of desolation in ball park upper decks.

He is the center of attention when he turns a routine two-hopper to short into a base hit, when he cuts down wayward baserunners with his rocket launcher from left field and, yes, even when he does something as ordinary as tapping a ball back to the mound.

The date was June 21, and the Royals were in Milwaukee. Batting with the bases empty in the sixth inning, Bo nubbed a grounder back to Brewers pitcher Jay Aldrich, who flipped to first base for the final out of the inning. Bo took a few steps out of the batter's box, glared at the pitcher and broke his bat. Over his helmet.

On the Royals' bench, Jackson's teammates went crazy. "You know, I asked Bo about it later," George Brett said, "and he said the bat was already cracked. So don't tell anyone. It's supposed to be a secret."

Bo added to his legend by breaking bats over his thigh on May 9 against Cleveland and on August 13 against Toronto. After Bo reduced his first bat to kindling, reporters swarmed his locker after the game, asking whether he'd ever done it before.

"I broke an aluminum bat over my knee in college," Bo said as reporters scribbled furiously. "Naw," Jackson went on, "just kidding."

NOBODY HAS EVER CONSIDERED MAJOR LEAGUE BASEBALL TO BE A SPOT FOR "ON THE JOB TRAINING" OF A SEMI-RAW RECRUIT... BUT THAT WAS BEFORE BO JACKSON CAME ALONG. NOT ONLY HAS HE REMAINED IN THE MAJORS, BUT HE HAS DEVELOPED INTO ONE OF THE GAME'S SUPERSTARS. HE BECOMES MORE SAVVY AND DANGEROUS WITH EACH PASSING PITCH...

...NOT THAT HE WAS EXACTLY A SLOUCH TO BEGIN WITH! WITNESS THIS EXCHANGE WITH ONE OF HIS "TUTORS", SEATTLE'S MIKE MOORE—

IT WAS HIS FIRST MAJOR LEAGUE HOME RUN!

...IT ALSO HAPPENED TO BE THE LONGEST HOMER IN THE HISTORY OF ROYALS STADIUM!

AND, OF COURSE, THERE WAS "*THE THROW*"...

SEATTLE VS. KANSAS CITY, TENTH INNING, SCORE TIED 3-3; HAROLD REYNOLDS TAKES OFF FROM FIRST ON A BLAST TO THE LEFT-FIELD CORNER BY SCOTT BRADLEY. REYNOLDS HAS ALREADY ROUNDED THIRD BY THE TIME BO CATCHES THE CAROM OFF THE WALL. THE PLAY — AND THE GAME — SHOULD BE OVER.

— BUT IT'S NOT!!!

OFF-BALANCE, FLAT-FOOTED, WITH ONE FOOT ON THE WARNING TRACK, BO'S ARM LETS LOOSE LIKE A CANNON —

...THE BALL HURTLES ACROSS THE OUTFIELD, PAST THE THIRD BASEMAN, *AND KEEPS ON GOING*....

...THROUGH THE INFIELD, PAST THE PITCHER, *AND KEEPS ON GOING*...

OVER 300 FEET...

...DIRECTLY INTO THE WAITING MITT OF BOB BOONE!!!

EVEN MORE AMAZING, IT WAS A STRIKE ON THE OUTSIDE CORNER !!! EVERYONE WAS ASTOUNDED — **ESPECIALLY** HAROLD REYNOLDS !

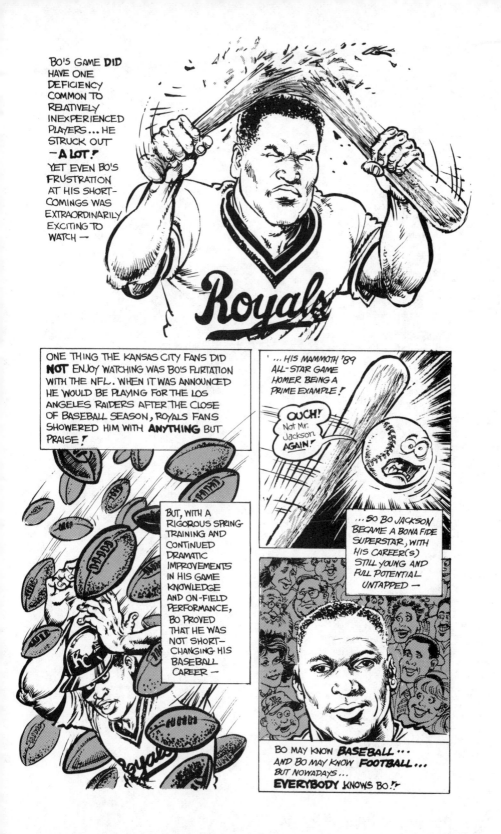

BO'S GAME **DID** HAVE ONE DEFICIENCY COMMON TO RELATIVELY INEXPERIENCED PLAYERS... HE STRUCK OUT —A LOT! YET EVEN BO'S FRUSTRATION AT HIS SHORT-COMINGS WAS EXTRAORDINARILY EXCITING TO WATCH —

ONE THING THE KANSAS CITY FANS DID **NOT** ENJOY WATCHING WAS BO'S FLIRTATION WITH THE NFL. WHEN IT WAS ANNOUNCED HE WOULD BE PLAYING FOR THE LOS ANGELES RAIDERS AFTER THE CLOSE OF BASEBALL SEASON, ROYALS FANS SHOWERED HIM WITH **ANYTHING** BUT PRAISE!

'... HIS MAMMOTH '89 ALL-STAR GAME HOMER BEING A PRIME EXAMPLE!

OUCH! Not Mr. Jackson AGAIN!

... SO BO JACKSON BECAME A BONA FIDE SUPERSTAR, WITH HIS CAREER(S) STILL YOUNG AND FULL POTENTIAL UNTAPPED —

BUT, WITH A RIGOROUS SPRING TRAINING AND CONTINUED DRAMATIC IMPROVEMENTS IN HIS GAME KNOWLEDGE AND ON-FIELD PERFORMANCE, BO PROVED THAT HE WAS NOT SHORT-CHANGING HIS BASEBALL CAREER —

BO MAY KNOW **BASEBALL** ... AND BO MAY KNOW **FOOTBALL** ... BUT NOWADAYS ... **EVERYBODY** KNOWS BO!!

BO KNOWS FOOTBALL, TOO

The announcement, which came in July 1987, was a bombshell.

Bo Jackson was having a good-news, bad-news season for the Kansas City Royals, the American League baseball team with whom he had signed 13 months earlier after spurning a whopping offer from the Tampa Bay Buccaneers of the National Football League. At the major league All-Star break in '87, Jackson boasted totals of 18 home runs and 45 runs batted in for the Royals. However, he had struck out a staggering 115 times in 81 games.

Just three months after reiterating his intentions of having a baseball-only professional career — he had fashioned a sign for reporters that read, "Don't be stupid and ask any football questions" — Bo jolted the Royals by agreeing to a five-year contract with the Los Angeles Raiders. No, Bo wasn't changing careers. Instead, he was adding one.

In Bo's mind, though, it was simpler than that. The 1985 Heisman Trophy winner said he merely wanted to give pro football a try.

"It's a hobby," Jackson said of his return to the football wars. "I wish I could make money fishing (another hobby). Those are my feelings. I can't express what somebody wants me to say. I say what Bo feels.

"Everything's been great, really. I'm having fun playing baseball, and I'll continue to have fun. There's no reason anyone should doubt that."

□

When Bo Jackson made his first appearance at the Los Angeles Raiders' headquarters at El Segundo, Calif., in the fall of 1987, there were skeptics all around. They surrounded him wherever he went. On the field. In the locker room. In the dining room. In the weight room.

They snickered, likely thinking to themselves: "So, this is Bo. Let's see how good this guy really is, this guy who thinks he can play two professional sports."

Although he was the No. 1 selection in the entire NFL draft in 1986, Bo arrived for duty with the Raiders as a seventh-round choice. While Tampa Bay had made him the draft's top pick in '86, Bo's refusal to sign with the Buccaneers over the course of a year's time made him eligible for selection again in '87. And the Raiders wisely invested a mid-to-low draft choice on him.

"He comes in and we're saying to each other, 'OK, show us what you got. We'll show you that football is no hobby for anyone,'" said Mike Haynes, veteran cornerback.

"We had heard how fast and strong he was, but we had to see it for ourselves," Haynes continued. "Then, on the first play of practice, he took

Bo Jackson and his agent, attorney Richard Woods, answer questions during the July 1987 press conference in which baseball star Bo explained his plans to take up a new hobby — professional football with the NFL's Los Angeles Raiders.

a simple pitch and ran around the corner so fast that I couldn't believe my eyes. He was a blur. I actually had to rub my eyes. I was astonished at his speed. I mean a-ston-ished. Everyone was.

"Now I have been around a lot of great football players and athletes (Haynes broke into the NFL in 1976). I've always been so used to getting good position on running backs to make the play and bring them down. All of them. There aren't many that have been able to elude me. Or out-smart me. Or out-power me. Or out-finesse me.

"But against Bo, forget it. The guy is obviously unstoppable. He's just too big and too fast for us cornerbacks to bring down. Linebackers, too. I've never seen an athlete like him before. And it'll be a long time before we ever see anything like him."

□

Zeph Lee has a vivid recollection of Bo's arrival on the pro football scene.

"Everyone was anticipating him running, especially me," said Lee, a Raiders running back at the time who since has been converted into a defensive back. While Lee stood on the sideline, Raiders cornerback Mike Haynes walked over to him.

"How fast can he run?" Haynes asked.

"At the (scouting) combine camp, they said he could run a 4.16," Lee replied. "He was timed off four different watches."

"Doubt it," Haynes said. ". . . 4.16? Too fast for a guy that big."

Just then, Bo took a pitch.

"We call it '18 flip,' " Lee said.

With the grace and fluidity of a dancer, Bo glided outside.

"The corner had containment," Lee said. "It's hard to break contain-ment once the corner comes up, whether you're running inside or out-side."

From the 40-yard line, Bo sliced inside, veered outside again and then sped out of sight.

"No one was within 20 yards of him," Lee said.

Seconds later, as Bo crossed the goal line, Haynes turned to Lee.

"Yeah, 4.16 is about right," Haynes cracked.

□

"We were having this one-on-one drill," said linebacker Jerry Robin-son, reflecting on Bo's debut in a pro-football practice session. "And Bo jumps up (to volunteer). So I jump up, too, saying, 'Let me take Bo.'

"So, Bo comes out and I'm thinking I'm doing a good job of getting up

Bo (right) with new Los Angeles teammate Marcus Allen after joining the Raiders in October 1987.

on him. Then he starts running out. At this point, I'm still close to him.

"Then he ran out and up and, with his head turned toward me, he was laughing and waving 'bye-bye' as he was running past me.

"He did something no one's ever done to me before."

□

"It's hard to believe he's playing two sports and doing so great at both. He's a guy who can win the Most Valuable Player award in both leagues (baseball's American League and the National Football League). In the same season. It'll happen someday. Watch."
                                                    —defensive back Zeph Lee, on Bo Jackson

□

On a dark and gloomy day, quarterback Steve Beuerlein guided the Raiders' offense during a practice session.

Jackson stood three yards behind him.

Beuerlein took a snap from center Don Mosebar, faked a pitch to Bo, backpedaled into the pocket and rolled to his left.

Bo made a turn in the shape of a "C" and headed across the middle of the field, his eyes on Beuerlein. Beuerlein eyed Bo and fired a 15-yard bullet. The pass was a little long and Bo had to dive for the ball. It deflected off his fingertips, fell to the ground and spun wildly before coming to a stop.

"Bo was lying on his stomach after missing the ball," Mike Haynes said. "Suddenly, in one motion, he turned over on his back and flipped up on his feet. Just like a gymnast.

"The guys who saw it couldn't believe their eyes. I turned to Lionel (Washington, a Raiders cornerback) and said, 'Did you see that?' He said, 'Yeah, but I'm not sure what I saw really happened.'

"It was like an optical illusion, seeing a 235-pound running back do that," Haynes said. "That's the thing, the incident, that's amazed me most about Bo. He flipped right up on his feet like a guy who's 5-foot-7, not 6-1, 235. His athletic ability is incredible. I don't think he really knows how good he is. Or how good he can become."

□

Raiders running back Steve Strachan played against Bo Jackson in college. Strachan was a Boston College Eagle, Jackson an Auburn Tiger. They met in a postseason game, the 1982 Tangerine Bowl.

Strachan was concluding his sophomore year. Bo was coming off a freshman season in which he had rushed for 829 yards in 10 games.

Even at that juncture, it was evident that Bo was something special. Strachan, of course, was a fine player in his own right. But they were on different levels in those days. Strachan knew Bo was good. He just didn't realize how good.

"My first exposure to Bo as a Raider was his first day here in 1987," Strachan recalled. "It was my third year in the NFL. For those three years, everyone was accustomed to a certain speed, the quickness, in which the game was played.

"But the very first day Bo came in, he took a pitch, ran around the end and everybody there sat back in a daze, it seemed, and said, 'Man, he's going faster than anyone else.'

"It was evident that this guy was playing at a different speed than everybody else. It was hard to believe. There always have been fast guys in the league. But nothing like Bo.

". . . All he did was take a pitch and all of a sudden a new standard for speed and quickness was established in the NFL."

□

For most professional football players, practice is a drag. A real bore. Except when Bo Jackson is around.

He enlivens the drills, to say the least. Monotony? What monotony?

"One time during practice, Bo took a handoff and went off right tackle," Raiders linebacker Greg Townsend remembered. "I was closing in on Bo on one side and Matt Millen was closing in on Bo on the other side.

"We had him cornered. There wasn't any chance of him getting away. We had this much room to catch him," said Townsend, his hands spread about two feet apart.

Suddenly, Townsend and Millen were face to face, left with nothing but air to catch. Bo blew right in between them, leaving the players aghast, perplexed. Even embarrassed.

"Matt and I just looked at each other too astonished to talk," Townsend said.

"Finally, I asked him, 'Was that for real?' He didn't say anything. He just looked downfield, shaking his head."

□

Jerry Robinson was still in awe over a mesmerizing maneuver by Bo Jackson when he approached Bo on the sidelines after a Raiders practice.

"Hey, Bo, how fast do you do the 40?" asked Robinson, still a bit out of breath after Bo darted past him on a one-on-one pass route that turned into a colossal mismatch.

"As fast as I have to," Bo replied.

Robinson nodded and grinned.

"Yep, I believe it," he said.

Later, in the locker room, Bo told Robinson that he chased rabbits when he was a boy growing up in Alabama.

"And he said he ran them down, too," Robinson said in wonderment. "Ran them into the ground."

□

When Raiders guard Steve Wisniewski holds his block on an opponent, he's satisfied.

When Wisniewski prevents a quarterback sack, he's satisfied.

When he creates an opening for a running back to shoot through, gaining significant yardage, Wisniewski is satisfied.

With Bo Jackson around, Wisniewski sometimes is not satisfied.

"Sometimes I'm not needed," said Wisniewski, a Raiders rookie lineman in 1989. "Sometimes nobody's needed. Sometimes Bo does it all by himself."

Case in point from the '89 season: Raiders vs. New England, second quarter, Los Angeles' ball, first and 10 at the Raiders' 35.

" 'Flip 19' was the play," Wisniewski said. "I'm supposed to work wide toward the sideline. My job is to hook the nose tackle.

"As Bo worked toward my way, I had to put a simple block on my guy. But before I could even hook my guy, Bo was already past me, long gone. I'm on my guy, holding him, ready to get him wide and I see this flash. It's Bo.

"I stopped and said to myself, 'Not again. Bo's done it again.' "

□

Brent Williams is a tough critic. The rugged defensive end doesn't pass out compliments to NFL opponents very often.

Williams, who played his fourth NFL season in 1989, doesn't even consider Bo Jackson a great running back. Just a good running back.

"Longevity determines greatness," Williams said.

But don't think Williams isn't impressed with Bo, especially after what Bo did to Williams when the Raiders met up with the New England Patriots at the Los Angeles Coliseum on a blustery autumn day in November of '89.

"I had an open tackle on him on a particular play and I expected him to try to outrun me, go down or just run out of bounds," Williams said.

"But he stayed up and then gave me a forearm.

"That shocked me. I was impressed. Most running backs don't do that, or wouldn't do that, especially a part-time running back who considers football his hobby. You figure that a guy who has to worry about two sports wouldn't throw a forearm into someone's helmet and jeopardize his career by breaking his arm.

"Regardless, it was a very gutsy play. It showed me a lot of courage. It showed me he's taking this business seriously. I wasn't sure of that before."

□

Bo can run with the football—everyone knows that.

The next logical question is: Can he catch it as well?

"He can. You can be sure of that," Raiders Coach Art Shell said.

In the first quarter of the Raiders-Patriots game in 1989, quarterback Steve Beuerlein took the snap and, as he dropped back into the pocket, Jackson ran out of the backfield, curved inside and headed for the middle of the field. Beuerlein rifled a line-drive pass.

The ball and Bo merged. New England free safety Fred Marion was right there, too.

As Bo snagged the ball like an All-Pro wide receiver, Marion made a vicious hit on him. Jackson bobbled the ball, but held on.

"I really laid into him," Marion said. "That was a big hit. For Bo to hold on to the ball like that was damn impressive, especially since he bobbled it. That was amazing.

"I can't say enough about the guy. He's magnificent. I gave him my best shot and he held on. That says it all. He runs. He catches. He's special."

□

On a sun-splashed Sunday at the Los Angeles Memorial Coliseum midway through the 1989 season, the Los Angeles Raiders were playing the defending American Football Conference champion Cincinnati Bengals.

It was early in the game and the Raiders had the ball, first and 10 at their 8-yard line.

Bo Jackson clapped his hands and casually walked a few steps to his designated spot, three yards behind Raiders quarterback Jay Schroeder. He twisted his body, bending down in a three-point stance.

"Everybody knew the play was called for Bo and everybody knows—knows now, at least—that when Bo gets the ball, anything can happen, no matter how far away you are from the goal line, 50 yards, 75 yards or 98 yards," Raiders tight end Mike Dyal said. "We were all kind of excited. We're always excited when Bo's getting the ball."

Even when the Raiders are 92 yards away from a touchdown.

Schroeder called the signals, took the snap, turned and handed off to Bo. Bo swept around left end and kept veering outside. He cut inside, then bolted outside, narrowly avoiding a hit from Bengals cornerback Lewis Billups. Bo sped to Los Angeles' 30-yard line, then the 40, then he turned it on, sprinting out of sight from the rest of the 21 players on the field, who watched in awe.

From the time he touched the ball, Bo never was touched by a Bengals player.

"He's a phenomenal athlete, a super, super talent," Dyal said. "He took the ball and did what most players only dream about."

Cincinnati Coach Sam Wyche had an opinion, too, after Bo's 92-yard sprint, the longest touchdown run in Raiders history.

"Bo is as advertised," Wyche said. "He is one of those rare ones that come along only so often. I hope everyone enjoys watching him now, because he will go down as one of the legends of the game."

□

Rickey Dixon, the highly regarded Cincinnati defensive back, had never been taken to school like he was on November 5, 1989.

The teacher: Bo Jackson.

What Jackson did was beat Dixon badly on the play that turned out to be Bo's much-acclaimed 92-yard touchdown jaunt.

"What can you say? He's absolutely one of the greatest players to ever put a uniform on. Forget that this is his third year," Dixon said. "Forget that he plays football only part-time. The guy is the greatest back I've played against. He's flat-out the best I've seen.

"Give him a seam and it's like someone shot him out of a cannon. The man is fast. I mean fast. F-a-s-t. You'd never know it by looking at him. I mean, the guy's 235 pounds. He's one big man. But he's the best in the game.

"They used to say Eric Dickerson was the best. No more. Bo is, without a doubt. I learned that today. I learned my lessons today.

"He let me know where I stand. And it's nowhere near him. I'm known as a damn good corner, one of the best in the league. But Bo made me look foolish. He did it to Mike Harden (while Harden was with the Denver Broncos). He did it to Boz (Seattle linebacker Brian Bosworth). He'll do it to everybody. The guy is simply the best."

Dixon was stationed at the left-corner position when Bo took a handoff and set sail on his long-distance journey.

"I was on the strongside," Dixon said. "Bo took the handoff and swept the weakside. I followed him, eyeing him the whole way. I knew he was fast. But never that fast. I sneaked over quickly to that side. I was planning to take the inside angle and cut him down. But once he cut back and hit the seam, it was like someone shot him out of a cannon. There was nothing to do at that point but to watch him, be in awe of him and admire his backside.

"A lot of guys around the league were saying Bo was faster than Willie Gault (the Raiders' wide receiver), but we didn't believe it. At least I didn't. Now I do. I'd love to see those two guys race. If they ran, I'd bet on Bo.

"There are a lot of great players in all sports. In basketball, there are Magic Johnson, Larry Bird, Michael Jordan. In hockey, there's (Wayne) Gretzky. Those guys play on another level. That's what Bo does here.

"If you hold him to 100 or 125 yards and a touchdown, you've contained him. That's saying something. He's in another class. He's rewriting the description of what a running back is. What's scary is that this is only his third year."

What Rickey Dixon didn't mention about the '89 Bengals-Raiders game was a touchdown run that came two possessions before Bo Jackson's bolt from the Los Angeles 8.

With the ball at the Cincinnati 7 and the game approximately 3½ minutes old, Jackson took a handoff and zoomed up the middle. The Bengals' Dixon latched on—for the ride. Bo carried the defender the last four yards into the end zone.

□

Few people were more impressed by Bo Jackson's 92-yard touchdown run against the Cincinnati Bengals in '89 than Raiders cornerback Mike Haynes.

"The guy continues to amaze me," Haynes said. "He's done the extraordinary. Impossible as it seems, he's getting better.

"That 92-yard run was something we may never see again—the way Bo did it, I mean. It just doesn't happen. It won't happen.

"He takes the pitch. OK, no big deal. He sweeps around the end. No big deal. But then you start to see something that you've never seen before. You see him break, then accelerate and accelerate and become a blur. It was like everyone was in slow motion except for Bo.

"He was as fluid as anyone could imagine, as graceful as anyone could imagine. But the thing that might have amazed me more than anything on that play was that most guys would get tight near the end of a run like that, especially carrying all that equipment. Not Bo.

"Think about that. He didn't get tight at all. Little guys, guys 5-9, 180, they get tight. Bo didn't. Amazing.

"Heck, he wasn't even out of breath after scoring. That's something."

Jackson even had enough energy after the touchdown gallop to engage in some end-zone showmanship, much to the delight of the crowd of 50,000-plus. He imitated a cowboy, whipping imaginary guns out of an imaginary holster, firing a few shots, blowing away some smoke and then sticking the guns back in the holster.

"I'm telling you, this guy is a living legend, a one-of-a-kind player," Haynes said. "He's in absolutely tremendous shape. I've never seen anyone in better shape. The only player who comes close to him, speed-wise, was O.J. Simpson, and O.J was only 204 pounds. O.J. wasn't going to run over you, just by you and away from you.

"Bo can run over you and around you. He's the ultimate threat."

□

Legendary touchdown runs are becoming rather common for Bo Jackson.

"Every time he touches the ball now, everybody gets the feeling that he can break it," said Al LoCasale, Raiders executive assistant.

The first time people got that feeling was on a Monday night at Seattle in 1987. The occasion was a Raiders-Seahawks game, only the fifth contest in Bo's National Football League career.

Entering that nationally televised fray, the Raiders' record for rushing yards on one carry was 89, established by Kenny King in a 1980 game against the San Diego Chargers, and the club mark for one game was 200, achieved by Clem Daniels in a 1963 game against the New York Jets.

"That's the night (November 30, 1987) Bo Jackson put himself on the map as one of the game's greatest players of all time—already," said line-backer Greg Townsend, who at that juncture was winding down his fifth season with the Raiders.

From the Raiders' 9-yard line, Bo took a pitch from quarterback Marc Wilson, cut outside and raced down the sideline like a thoroughbred.

"He ran so fast that it appeared everyone else was in slo-mo," Townsend said of the second-quarter burst.

Bo kept running, too—right into the end zone, then into the tunnel underneath the stands. Where was he going, anyway? To Canton?

"That's where he'll end up," Townsend said. "He's phenomenal. He's something I've never seen before. He's something no one's seen before.

"We thought we saw the best in Jim Brown. Then Walter Payton. The best is Bo.

"That touchdown run in Seattle, well, let's just say that it had to be one of the greatest runs in the history of football. Why? Because so many guys had angles on him and he outran everyone.

There was no peace for the newest Raider star in 1987 as he was besieged by the press after almost every game.

"Boz (Seattle linebacker Brian Bosworth) has good speed. He had an angle on Bo. And Bo easily beat him. He really blew right past him. Kenny Easley (Seahawks defensive back) had a good angle on Bo. But Bo blew right past him. I couldn't believe what I was seeing when he did that. No one could.

"When he was running down the sideline, it wasn't like he was a football player. It was like he was a track star. With that run, he showed everyone who he was and what he was capable of. And he's obviously capable of doing things no one else has done before. Not Jim Brown. Not Gale Sayers. Not O.J. Simpson. Not Earl Campbell. Bo is incredibly special. That's all there is to it.

"The only run that I can compare it to was Marcus Allen's 'U-turn' run that he turned into a touchdown in the Super Bowl (January 1984, against the Washington Redskins). And the only reason why I compare it (Allen's 74-yard sprint) is because Marcus' was done in the biggest game of the season.

"When I stood on the sidelines watching Bo's 91-yard run, I turned to defensive end Howie Long and said, 'Yeah. This guy can play in this league.'"

Earlier in the second period, Jackson had scored against the Seahawks on a 14-yard pass from Wilson. Then, 3½ minutes into the third quarter, Bo got into the end zone on a two-yard run.

By night's end, Jackson not only had smashed King's record for the longest run by a Raider, but he also had broken Daniels' mark for one game. He finished with 221 yards on 18 carries as the Raiders frolicked, 37-14.

Not bad for someone who five weeks earlier had never played a down of professional football.

□

Bo Jackson has become a nationwide phenomenon.

Everywhere he goes, people stop and look. They watch his every move.

At Houston's Astrodome, for instance, Bo had a police escort as he entered the facility for the 1989 Raiders-Oilers game.

"He's a celebrity," Raiders linebacker Greg Townsend said. "When someone is doing something that no one else is doing, people want to see him. Get a look at him up close to see if he's for real."

Besides the onlookers in enemy stadiums, there are banners. And more banners.

Spotted at the Astrodome, known as the "House of Pain," was a banner reading "Bo Don't Know Pain." There also was a "Bo's Not Going To Do Diddley" sign.

In Philadelphia, there was a "Bo Doesn't Know Whitney" banner, alluding to singer Whitney Houston, who reportedly had been seen with Eagles quarterback Randall Cunningham.

"I can't recall ever going to an opposing stadium and seeing so many banners for a guy on the other team," said Raiders quarterback Steve Beuerlein. "But that's the kind of attention Bo draws."

□

If you're wondering what Bo Jackson's next "hobby" might be, consider sprint-relay competition with some of his Raider teammates.

"He's talked about it," said the fastest Raider of them all, former Olympic gold medalist Sam Graddy.

"He says it'd be a lot of fun, and I agree with him," said Graddy, a wide receiver from Tennessee. "If the NFL ever decided to have an off-season competition, and decided to have relay teams, we'd love it. Each team could enter their four fastest guys.

"We'd enter Bo, me, Willie (Gault) and either Terry McDaniel or Zeph

Lee. Bo gets a kick out of that every time we talk about it. He says we'd burn some rubber."

☐

"It is incumbent upon us as people, as historians, as athletes and as fans, to take in and cherish the extraordinary ability and talent of Bo Jackson because I don't think we'll see a running back of his magnitiude, grace, speed, power and excitement for quite some time."

—Vince Evans

No, Vince Evans isn't a politician. He has been a professional quarterback for more than a decade, spending the bulk of his time with the Chicago Bears but also playing in the United States Football League and then serving as a backup with the Los Angeles Raiders.

"For the people living today, we'll probably never see someone of Bo Jackson's caliber and greatness in our lifetime," Evans said. "He is a guy who, when you look back at history, comes along once every century."

Considering Evans' lofty regard for the talents of one Vincent Edward Jackson, it's hardly surprising that Bo has left the veteran quarterback speechless on several occasions.

"Things I never even dreamed about seeing, he's done," Evans said. "He's run over guys bigger than him. He's run around guys supposedly quicker than him.

"He's really an amazing running back. I played with Walter Payton when I was with the Bears and I've never seen anything approaching Bo's status or level. There simply aren't enough superlatives to fully describe his presence and talent.

"That 92-yard run he had against Cincinnati (in 1989) was so spectacular, I can't even begin to describe the magnitude, the ramifications, of such a run. For him to go untouched on a play like that was just incredible. Really incredible. I never saw a guy move away from people like that.

"Never have I seen a guy run so long and so fast. He never got tired on that TD run. He was down there in 10 seconds flat. With all that equipment on.

"He is so unbelievably fast, and so unbelievably strong, that he's virtually unstoppable in most situations."

☐

Looking up at the bright blue Southern California sky, Mike Harden could hardly believe what had happened to him.

What was that silver-and-black streak that flattened him like a Mack truck?

What was the license plate of that vehicle?

Number 34, Bo Jackson.

Harden was Bo's first major highlight-film victim. He became a symbol—a symbol of what could happen if you found yourself in Bo's path.

"The hit looked much worse than it really was, but I was pretty embarrassed," Harden said, "especially when I saw it (on a replay) up on the scoreboard."

The situation was this: November 22, 1987. The Los Angeles Raiders playing host to the Denver Broncos. Bo Jackson participating in his fourth National Football League game. A crowd of 60,000-plus on hand at the Los Angeles Memorial Coliseum.

"Part of my problem," said Jackson, alluding to less-than-sensational performances in his first three NFL games, "is that I'm six pounds heavier and a step slower than when I was in college . . . Can I get it back? I don't know. None of us is getting any younger.

". . . Today (against the Broncos) I said to hell with running around people," continued Jackson, still eight days from his 25th birthday. "I'll run over them."

It was midway through the second quarter when Bo made good on his vow. Los Angeles had the ball on the Denver 35-yard line and Marcus Allen, the up back in the I-formation, went in motion to the right. Quarterback Marc Wilson took the snap and pitched to Jackson, who was trailing Allen. Bo took only one step to the right, however, then planted his left foot. He pivoted 180 degrees and headed back toward the left.

One Bronco didn't take the misdirection fake—cornerback Harden. He held his ground at the 30 and readied himself for a hit on Jackson that would have held the Raiders' back to a five-yard gain. It was Bo, though, who wound up doing the hitting.

Jackson lowered his helmet and drove it into Harden's chest. In the words of one national sportswriter, "Harden went over on his back as if he had been poleaxed." Bo roared on, all the way to the end zone.

"I expected Jackson to . . . shake me down, to try to get me off-balance so he could run around me," Harden said after the game.

"Like I said," Bo observed, "I was experimenting this afternoon, trying to figure out whether I should run around people or over them. I decided to go over him (Harden)."

□

Mike Harden says his famous crash—er, clash—with Bo Jackson in 1987 wasn't quite as bad as it appeared.

Denver cornerback Mike Harden (31) prepares to put a hit on Bo Jackson during a November 1987 game at the Los Angeles Coliseum. Bo ran over Harden like a Mack truck and rambled 35 yards, diving into the end zone (below) for his first NFL touchdown.

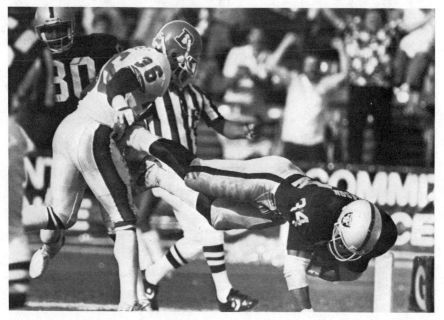

"When I see a guy running with the ball, I come up to hit," Harden explained. "With the play being in the open field, it's a little different. There's a lot of room to move and there's no one around to help, no one around to alter the play, change someone's direction.

"When Bo came toward me, he made a cut, as if he was going to go around me."

That move proved pivotal.

"When he made that cut, he got me off-balance," Harden said. "If I hadn't gone for the fake, I would have had my balance. On a play like that, balance means everything. It's the difference between making the play and not making the play."

It's also the difference between remaining on your feet or winding up flat on your back.

"Just when I thought he was going to go around me, he ducked his head and hit me high in the chest," recounted Harden, who would become Jackson's teammate on the Raiders in 1989. "Since I didn't have my feet planted, and was off-balance, his incredible power—combined with his devastating speed—just knocked me over.

"The hit looked a lot worse than it was. I wasn't hurt. I just happened to be a guy caught in an awkward situation. I was in the open field with a great back and got the worst end of it."

The very worst.

☐

"Bo is God's gift to halfbacks. He's unreal. He's a step beyond stupendous. He was destined to be a football player."
—Lester Hayes, Raiders' cornerback, 1977-1986

☐

"For the first time in a long time, I get chills down my spine when I watch someone else do something on a football field."
—Raiders defensive end Howie Long,
talking about Bo Jackson during
Jackson's rookie season in the NFL

☐

"It's as if the deity said, 'I want to make an athletic body' and, poof, he made Bo. The guy has a perfect, God-given physique."
—Todd Christensen, longtime Raiders tight end

"I think he's the most awe-some physical specimen I've ever seen."

　　　　　　　　—Howie Long

☐

Bob Golic, the Raiders' animated and comedic nose tackle, was resting on the bench when Bo Jackson began his 92-yard touchdown run against Cincinnati in the fall of 1989.

Getting a breather before the next defensive series, Golic sat with his head lowered. As he heard the fans' screams heighten, and saw his teammates on the sidelines converge in one big cluster, his head rose slowly, then his body.

"I obviously had to drag myself up and see what was going on," Golic said.

He had an idea what was happening.

"Had to be something to do with Bo," he figured.

Golic caught the last 50 yards of Bo's journey into the Raiders' record book.

Former Raider star Lester Hayes is a certified member of Bo Jackson's growing fan club.

"I caught a glimpse of him when everyone—everyone except Bo—was huffing and puffing," Golic said. "I'm sure I know what those linemen, linebackers and cornerbacks were saying while watching Bo dust them. 'Why waste the energy? He's gone. Couldn't catch him for miles.' "

Before the '89 season, Golic had seen Bo only on tape.

"Never live. Never up front. Never in person," said the former New England Patriots and Cleveland Browns player.

When he saw Bo for the first time "in real life," Golic's jaw dropped a notch or two.

"I never saw a back so big outrunning cornerbacks who do 4.3's and 4.4's (in the 40)," Golic said. "But Bo was blowing right past them. They had no chance. None whatsoever. It was a gas watching this machine."

□

Back home in Warner Robins, Ga., Raiders safety Eddie Anderson and his friends used to chase turkeys around the farm.

"Never could catch one easy," he said. "They're shifty creatures."

Anderson said trying to catch Bo Jackson is akin to trying to catch a turkey.

"I was watching him one day in practice, running from sideline to sideline," Anderson said. "He started off slow, then ran faster and faster and faster.

"The last few sprints, he was like a blur. I'm saying, 'This can't be. He can't be that fast.'

"Then during practice, he really turned on the burners. What amazed me most is how he was able to change speeds, change gears, just like a car. He was like a Porsche and everyone else was a Volkswagen.

"No one could catch him. He was like a wild turkey, with everyone chasing after him, and no one having enough speed or quickness to get him."

□

When Bo Jackson cut back, stutter-stepped, escaped the line of scrimmage and then broke two tackles, it appeared he was headed for another National Football League touchdown of the 90-yard variety.

"He might go!!" ESPN analyst Joe Theismann yelled into his microphone on the night of November 12, 1989.

Suddenly, San Diego Chargers safety Vencie Glenn stretched out, got his left hand on Bo's left foot and tripped up the Los Angeles Raiders' back, thus preventing Jackson from recording his third 90-yard scoring run in 22 games as a professional and his second such sprint in successive weeks. The week before, Bo had traveled 92 yards against Cincinnati.

When Bo walked off the field at San Diego Jack Murphy Stadium, he was met at the sidelines by Raiders Coach Art Shell.

"What the hell's going on?" asked Shell, breaking into a wide grin. "You had a chance to break another long one. What happened?"

"Can't break 'em all, Coach," Bo replied. "Gotta mix in a few 20-yard gains every now and then."

□

The day's mail had just arrived. Frank (Monte) Montecalvo, a Raiders staff assistant, spread the letters out on his desk inside the lobby of the team's headquarters.

There were 15 piles of mail. One stack was higher than the rest.

"This pile's just for Bo," Montecalvo said of the four-inch-high stack.

There was a time when Marcus Allen, Howie Long and Willie Gault received the most mail.

"It was so close between them you couldn't call it," Montecalvo said. "Then Bo came in and passed them all. Now, it's no contest."

□

For a solid week, the New England defense studied films of Bo Jackson in preparation for the Patriots-Raiders game in the 12th week of the 1989 season.

"We watched every run, every catch, everything he did," Patriots safety Roland James said. "Watched it again and again."

The Patriots were in awe.

"With a back like Bo, a guy who's so big and so strong, you have to get all 11 guys after him to make sure he doesn't go too far," said Patriots defender Fred Marion.

Marion and James received a dose of Bo's sheer power and strength in the final period of the Raiders' 24-21 victory over New England.

After taking a handoff, Bo bashed his way up the middle, through the front line, past linebackers Vincent Brown and Lawrence McGrew and into Marion and James. He rammed into them and pushed them four yards back before they were able to bring him down.

"I was shocked by his strength and force," Marion said. "Really shocked. The guy is built like no other running back on earth."

"Running backs don't do what he did on that play," James said. "He's got great legs, great leverage. If you hit him high, he'll carry you three-four yards. You have to hit him low."

But, advised Raiders safety Vann McElroy, don't hit him in his thigh "because he could break your shoulder."

Concluded Marion: "The thing about Bo is that when you go after him, you better bring your best hit with you, and even then, you better be prepared to take a lick, too."

□

Like Bo Jackson, Jay Schroeder knows football. Like Bo, Schroeder knows baseball, too.

Schroeder was the third player taken in the first round of baseball's amateur free-agent draft in June 1979. He was chosen by the Toronto Blue Jays.

"In a way, I know what Bo's going through. In a way I don't," said

Schroeder, who has spent five seasons as a National Football League quarterback with the Washington Redskins and the Los Angeles Raiders. "I
didn't play both sports—on this level—at the same time.

"To me, it's extraordinary that he's doing it. I'm astonished. I really
don't think people understand what he's doing. I don't think they comprehend the magnitude of excellence he's reached—in two sports at the same
time. I don't think they realize what an extraordinary feat this is."

Schroeder, in fact, had finished his professional baseball career before
playing a down in the NFL. Primarily an outfielder, he never rose above
the Class A ranks in the Blue Jays' organization. Bo, on the other hand,
entered pro baseball at the Class AA level.

"What's phenomenal about Bo is that he takes a few days off (after the
baseball season) and is able to jump right into another sport without missing a beat," Schroeder said. "Plus, he plays at the top of his game in both
sports . . . He's up there with the superstars of the game.

"He can hit a baseball out of sight and can run for 90-yard touchdowns. He can steal 30 bases a year (Bo's big-league high actually is 27) and
plow four yards for a touchdown, carrying two guys on his back.

"He's blessed. I'd like to do what he's doing . . . I played in the Blue
Jays' minor league system for four years. I know how tough it is to make it
in baseball. To make it in two sports, like Bo has, is amazing."

□

Jay Schroeder's two-sport professional performance hardly matches
up with that achieved by NFL teammate Bo Jackson, but the two share one
baseball statistic. Neither athlete would boast about this number, however.

As a struggling player in the Class A Carolina League in 1982,
Schroeder struck out a whopping 172 times. Jackson, as a fast-emerging
major leaguer in 1989, was a strikeout victim on, yes, 172 occasions.
Schroeder's total led the Carolina League; Bo's topped the American
League.

□

Vann McElroy, the Los Angeles Raiders' hard-hitting and hard-nosed
safety, couldn't wait to get his hands on Bo Jackson.

"I wanted to introduce him to the NFL and the NFL's way of hitting,"
McElroy said with a sneer.

It was well into the 1987 NFL season when Jackson arrived at the
Raiders' headquarters to begin his professional football career. Only a
short time earlier, Bo had been playing for the Kansas City Royals.

Left field is a lot different than the backfield—few people will argue that. McElroy wanted to emphasize the difference right away. Indeed, he wanted to make a lasting impression about the hazards of engaging in play-for-pay football.

"I was really excited to drill him. Drill him good," McElroy said. "I wanted to knock him down. Really belt him around.

"Here he was, coming in from the major leagues, a rookie, saying all these things, thinking he could do it all. I resented it. A lot of guys did. I was saying to myself, 'I'll show him. I'll show him what the NFL's about.' "

Moments later, McElroy had his chance to nail Bo. From the 15-yard line, Bo took a pitch and ran left. McElroy had his eye on Bo all the way and moved in. He started to gain speed. He hunched his back. He lowered his head. He was ready for a collision.

Suddenly, Bo blew past McElroy—like Roadrunner, the cartoon character, turning on his jets and speeding past the coyote.

"I had never seen a guy explode by me like that before," McElroy said. "Never. I've seen fast running backs before, but Bo is in another class. He's all by himself.

"When I got close to him, I thought I had him. Suddenly, he was gone. I said, 'Jeez. How'd he do that?' Right then and there I knew this guy was something special.

"I was ready to floor him. I wanted to check his intestinal fortitide. Well, he showed me right away what he was made of."

Speed, power and determination, among other things.

□

"He's a cornerback's nightmare."

That's the oft-heard description of Bo Jackson around the National Football League.

"He's the talk of (defensive) backfields throughout the league," said San Diego Chargers cornerback Gill Byrd.

"When he turns the corner and is heading full speed at you, you're in trouble," said Cinncinnati Bengals corner Eric Thomas. "He's like a bull on the loose."

"There's really nothing you can do when he comes around the corner heading at you full speed—except pray," cracked Melvin Jenkins of the Seattle Seahawks.

"He's scary," Washington defender Alvin Walton acknowledged. "And I don't scare easily."

"How do you prepare for Bo?" said Cincinnati's Rickey Dixon. "You can study films day and night but once he gets in the open field, forget it. He's gone.

"The only way to stop him is to gang-tackle before he sees a seam. If he spots that seam, post that 'six' on the scoreboard."

□

Raiders linebacker Emanuel King has seen a lot of Bo Jackson.

"In college and the pros," said King, who played collegiately at Alabama.

So if anyone on the Raiders has the background to suggest that Bo is better now than he was in college, and keeps getting better as the years pass, it's King.

"Know what? Bo is better now than he's ever been," King said. "He seems to be getting better every season. He's more determined. He's better conditioned. He thrives on better competition and elevates his game, his performance, to a higher level."

King has seen Bo run wild. Jackson burned Alabama's defense for 256 yards rushing in the 1983 Auburn-Crimson Tide game, averaging 12.8 yards per carry in that contest.

King also has seen Bo blunder.

"I once saw him run the wrong way in college," King said, laughing. "Bo wouldn't make that mistake now. He's more mature. He's more professional. I haven't seen him make any mistakes since he's been with the Raiders.

"What amazes me most about Bo is his change of speed," King continued. "He doesn't look to be running fast, then he motors around a corner and shifts into another gear. I never realized Bo was this fast. He doesn't seem to be putting in any effort—until you look at other players trying to catch him. Then you know he's moving."

□

Art Shell has been part of professional football since 1968.

For 15 seasons, he anchored the offensive line for the Oakland and Los Angeles Raiders, playing in 207 league games and 23 playoff games, including eight American Football League/American Football Conference championship games and two Super Bowls (both of which the Raiders won).

An eight-time Pro Bowl participant, Shell was regarded as perhaps the best National Football League lineman of his era. After retiring following the 1982 season, he spent 6½ years as a Raiders assistant coach before ascending to the head position.

Through it all, Shell has seen some of football's greatest running backs perform. He figured it would be quite a while before anyone from the game's "new breed" made his select list.

Then Bo Jackson came along.

"He's an amazing man, truly a great football player," Shell said.

Shell still marvels at Bo's hammering of Denver defender Mike Harden in 1987.

"Bo just exploded through a seam," Shell said. "There was just one guy in his way—Harden. And Bo ran through him. Ran right over him. Just like a big, old truck.

"The people on the sidelines, well, we just couldn't believe what we saw. We kind of just looked at each other in awe. Bo displayed a speed and explosiveness that I had never seen in all my years in the NFL. He's unique. You can't compare him with anybody, and you certainly can't compare anyone with him."

□

There was a time when Raiders linebacker Linden King paid little attention to his team's offense during the course of a game.

He was too busy going over defensive strategies, plays, formations or just plain resting his weary bones on the bench.

Then Bo Jackson became a Raider and Linden King changed his ways. He began watching the offense.

"Bo's too exciting not to watch," King said. "Every time he touches the ball, he can go all the way. There are not many backs you can say that about.

"You have your upper echelon of the NFL—the Eric Dickersons, the Herschel Walkers. But Bo? He's above that. Well above that. He plays on his own level, a level he created on his own.

"I'm glad he's on my team because if I was playing against him, I don't think there's anything I could do to stop him. And I'm 20 pounds heavier and three inches taller.

"... I've never seen anyone so fast and so strong. He's quick as a cat. Strong as a bull. When God was handing out talent, Bo got it all.

"When I watch him, I try to figure out ways to stop him. It's not easy. You have to realize what you're dealing with. Ability-wise, he's so far ahead of everybody in this game.

"Without a doubt, he's the best athlete I've ever seen. I've been around a few years (King made his NFL debut in 1978). I've played with and against a lot of great ballplayers. But Bo's a cut above."

□

When Howie Long, the Raiders' standout defensive end, talks about Bo Jackson, his eyes widen, his voice level decreases, his words are spoken slowly and carefully.

People have been in awe of Howie Long for years. Howie Long has been in awe of Bo Jackson from the moment he set eyes on him.

"We are seeing the future in Bo Jackson," he said.

Long paused and then added: "Ninety-yard touchdown runs. Outrunning fleet cornerbacks. Ramming into huge linebackers, driving them five yards backward."

He paused again, wearing an expression of disbelief.

"Come on. Never in my wildest dreams did I ever imagine a running back doing those things," he said. "There's no question that Bo Jackson is the athlete of our time. That sums it up. He is the athlete of our time. He's Jim Brown with speed. Awesome speed. He's Earl Campbell with speed.

"Every time he touches the ball, you get this eerie feeling, an exciting feeling, that he can break it. That's unusual. I've never experienced an emotion like that before. That's how special Bo is. . . .

Defensive end Howie Long, an imposing figure in his own right, is one of Bo's greatest admirers.

"Bo's ahead of his time. Everybody's time, for that matter. He is the future. We might not see anyone like him until the year 2010 or 2020."

□

Tim Goad, nose tackle of the New England Patriots, saw a flash. Then a blur.

"I didn't know what was happening," he said. "I thought my eyes were deceiving me."

With Bo Jackson darting around, such things have been known to occur.

What, in fact, occurred was this: Bo, having taken a pitch from quarterback Steve Beuerlein, straddled the line of scrimmage and looked for an opening. Spotting it, he cut back and squirted through the line for an 11-yard gain.

"That play impressed me more than anything Bo did during the game," Goad said of Jackson's performance in the Raiders' 1989 clash with the Patriots. "I got real good penetration on the play. I was right in the gap he was going to run through. But he read his blocks so well and so fast that he was behind me before I realized it.

"There was nothing I could do about it. Nothing. He was behind me in a flash. What made the run different from other runs was the incredible quickness of it. Really, I had never seen anyone break the line that fast. I didn't think it was possible to do it that quick.

"Bo is incredible—and that's an understatement. If he devoted himself to football full-time, there's no doubt in my mind that he'd be the greatest to ever play this game."

□

OK, Bo Jackson can do the glamour things. He can run and catch as a football player, and he can run, hit and throw as a baseball player.

But how adept is he at "trench" work, like blocking?

Just ask defensive back Roland James of the New England Patriots.

When James and the Patriots took on Bo and the Raiders during the 1989 season, Jackson was running interference on one play as reserve back Steve Smith moved swiftly around the left side of the New England defense.

James moved toward Smith, eagerly.

"I was preparing to hammer him," James said.

The hammer was applied, all right—by Bo Jackson. Slamming into James like a lineman, Bo not only prevented him from making the tackle on Smith, he also took James completely out of the play. The longtime Patriot was sent flying toward the sidelines.

"Great block," James said. "I didn't expect it. He came in high and hard. Perfect block. I couldn't do anything. There was no chance of getting Smith."

Said Smith: "That showed what a complete player Bo is. And it showed what an unselfish player Bo is. Usually, I'm the one who's blocking. When I took it in (from the 11 for a touchdown), Bo was far more excited that I scored than if he scored. That tells you a lot about Bo."

□

Raiders center Don Mosebar doesn't see much of Bo Jackson's face.

"Except in the huddle," Mosebar said.

**Bo talks things over with Philadelphia quarterback Randall Cunningham
after the Eagles' 10-7 victory over the Raiders in a 1989 matchup.**

"One thing I know better than anyone is Bo's, uh, uh, I'll say backside . . . I mostly see him running away from everyone downfield."
Mosebar laughed.

"The guy is faster than anyone I've ever seen," Mosebar said. "When
he gets going, forget it. I'm telling you, I know his backside better than his
face."

□

"He doesn't seem mortal at times."
—longtime NFL linebacker Linden King,
describing the multi-talents
of Bo Jackson

John Gesek, the Los Angeles Raiders' 6-foot-5, 275-pound guard, has seen Bo Jackson do some startling things on the football field.

"I've seen him run 90 yards for touchdowns, run over people, run through people, run around people and run past people," Gesek said. "I've seen him put some remarkable moves on players, completely faking them out. Leaving them embarrassed.

"One of the greatest things I've seen him do on the field was on a seven-yard touchdown run right up the middle against the Bengals."

Bo slammed into the Cincinnati line, broke two tackles at the Bengals' 5 and then ran into defender Rickey Dixon at the 4.

"We thought he was going down," Gesek said of Bo.

He was wrong.

"I think we all learned never to assume Bo is ever going to go down until he's down for sure," Gesek said.

Since Dixon failed to level Bo with a straight-on tackle, he hopped on Bo's back. What transpired for Dixon was a piggyback ride into the end zone.

"On that play, Bo . . . had nowhere to go," Gesek emphasized. "He was stopped not once but twice on the play. But he basically said, 'Screw it,' put his shoulder down, rammed into everyone in sight and went through them. He just pushed his way into the end zone.

"Not many guys can do that. Fullbacks, yes. Not many other running backs. Certainly not guys who can run as fast as Bo does. For most guys, scoring on a play like that is impossible.

"But with Bo, obviously nothing's impossible."

□

Week seven of the 1989 National Football League season found the Los Angeles Raiders in Philadelphia to play the Eagles, a team many pro football experts thought would reach the Super Bowl.

During the second period of a scoreless game at Veterans Stadium, ballcarrier Bo Jackson crashed into the line, squirted through a maze of arms and bodies, cut right, froze Eagles linebacker Seth Joyner with a head fake and burst upfield.

The end zone beckoned.

Forty-five yards later, Eagles cornerback Izel Jenkins, having a perfect angle, closed in on Jackson. He caught up to Bo—to the utter disbelief of many players. Shockingly, he even knocked Bo off his feet.

Bo is mortal, after all.

"When Bo got back to the huddle, we all stared at him," Raiders guard John Gesek recalled. "I said, 'Bo, what happened? What's wrong with you? You sick? Tired? You should have broken that thing for a touchdown easy.

Why didn't you just take that thing into the end zone, Bo? A lot of guys could have taken that into the end zone. Why didn't you? You're supposed to be the greatest?'"

Bo smiled and started to laugh.

"Didn't want to blow my hams (hamstrings)," he responded, cracking up everyone in the huddle. "Didn't want to turn on the afterburners just yet. I'm saving 'em."

☐

The first time Bo Jackson touched the football in a regular-season NFL game, it was a crisp autumn day in New England.

The place: Sullivan Stadium, Foxboro, Mass. The opponent: The New England Patriots.

"Naturally, we were all very excited," Raiders linebacker Greg Townsend said. "We knew what Bo could do. He showed us how extraordinary he was in practice. But we were all dying to see him do it in a game."

Jackson didn't disappoint his teammates or the Raiders' management.

Blasting off left tackle, Bo squeezed through a little hole, then burst through. He broke two tackles. Then he dragged Patriots cornerback Raymond Clayborn five yards.

Total haul: 14 yards.

"We were going crazy on the sidelines," Townsend said. "We knew right then and there that we had something special. Something very special. Sometime to behold and cherish.

"Had he run through a big, wide hole for 14 yards, well, it wouldn't have been such a big deal. But he spotted a little hole, cut back, changed his momentum, burst through, broke two tackles and dragged another guy five yards."

Ken Sims, New England defensive end and former No. 1 selection overall in the NFL draft, vividly remembers that introduction to Bo Jackson.

"When he burst through the seam, my heart seemed to come up to my throat," he said. "He had this look in his eyes. A fierce look. A hungry look. The look of an untamed tiger. He's scary."

☐

Brian Bosworth is, well, how to put this? Let's call him loquacious.

Usually, the Boz has the ability to back up what comes out of his mouth. Usually, but not always.

A case in point was when the Seattle Seahawks' linebacker went one-on-one with the Los Angeles Raiders' Bo Jackson at the Kingdome on a

Loquacious Seattle linebacker Brian Bosworth, alias "the Boz," was freight-trained by Bo in a 1987 goal-line confrontation.

Monday night in late November of 1987.

Los Angeles had possession at the Seahawks' 2 and the ball went to Bo. He stutter-stepped left, cut right and headed for the end zone. The only obstacle that could keep Bo from the goal line was the Boz.

This was theater. This was sheer excitement. This is what everyone wanted to see: Bo vs. Boz.

At the 1, they met. Actually, they collided. Jackson put his shoulder down and rammed into Bosworth. Resembling a bulldozer, Bo pushed Boz backward as if the Seattle defender were a lightweight. Touchdown!

"He just flat freight-trained my butt," Bosworth acknowledged. "He came up inside. I didn't know if he was going to cut back and run it inside or go outside. I hesitated for a second. That's all it took. He caught me off-balance."

For Seattle linebacker Tony Woods, the image of Bo plowing through the Boz is forever etched in his memory.

"I'll never forget it," he said. "It was remarkable. It showed what kind of brute strength, brute force, Bo had. For him to take on Boz and win, well, it was extraordinary."

After watching Jackson get the best of Bosworth, Seattle defensive end Jeff Bryant said (hopefully, no doubt), "Bo should stick to baseball."

□

For many years, Raiders executive Al LoCasale and cornerback Mike Haynes argued about who was the fastest player on the team. The cast of contenders would change periodically, but the LoCasale/Haynes debate raged on.

When Bo Jackson arrived, the arguing ceased.

"The first day Bo came in, Mike Haynes was standing next to me when Bo began running a play," LoCasale said. "He (Haynes) turned to me and said, 'No more arguments . . . now the argument is who's the second fastest.'"

LoCasale, who has been in professional football since 1960, was stunned that a man of Jackson's size could outrun everyone else on the Los Angeles squad.

"For a 235-pound guy to be the fastest guy on this team, well, it's pretty amazing," LoCasale said. "That's all I can say."

□

In the recorded history of the 70-year-old National Football League, only one player has run 90 or more yards from the line of scrimmage *twice.* That man accomplished the feat after playing in just 21 NFL games.

That man is Bo Jackson.

☐

O.J. Simpson would pay to see Bo Jackson carry the football.

"I'm a big fan of running backs, and Bo brings as much talent to the position as anyone in the history of the game," said Simpson, who rushed for 2,003 yards for the Buffalo Bills in 1973. "He's brought more talent to the position than I've ever seen, that's for sure.

"He's as fast as any running back who's ever played the game and he's bigger than all of them. When you walk into the stadium that Bo Jackson is going to be playing in, you know you're going to see a guy you might never see again as long as you live. You know you're going to see a guy who might do something you've never seen before, something that's never been done before.

The great O.J. Simpson says he would pay to see Bo Jackson carry a football.

"That's rare. There are guys you expect great performances from and guys you see that might do something that no one's ever dreamed of. Bo's one of those guys.

"You get that special feeling from Bo. That performance in Seattle (221 yards rushing, a 91-yard scoring run, the touchdown smash against Brian Bosworth and three TDs overall). Running down Mike Harden. That 92-yard run against Cincinnati.

"Those are things that are so special. He's a numbing performer. The way I've always viewed it is this: Every 10 years, a special runner comes along. Jim Brown. Gale Sayers. I'd like to think I was one. Eric Dickerson. Now Bo."

O.J. paused.

"But Bo has more tools than all of us," Simpson said. "He brings more talent to the position than anyone who has ever played this game or anyone who ever will."

□

Al LoCasale, Raiders executive assistant, is a big Bo Jackson fan. So is his 10-year-old son Nicholas.

Nicholas also is a big Oakland Athletics fan.

So when Bo Jackson and the Kansas City Royals made a West Coast swing in July 1989, LoCasale took Nicholas to the Oakland Coliseum to see Bo and the Royals play the A's.

"So what happens?" LoCasale said. "Bo hits two home runs. Every time he hits one, I jump up and start clapping. And there's my son next to me, yelling, 'Dad, come on. Knock if off. Knock it off.' "

LoCasale likes seeing Bo Jackson do well with the Royals. On the other hand, he's always eager for the Royals' season to end. The sooner the Royals are finished, the sooner Bo slips into a Raiders uniform.

"Regardless, we're rooting for Bo," LoCasale said. "We're very proud of what he's accomplishing—in both sports, not just football.

"Knowing the situation he's in, you're especially proud, because what he's doing is rare. What's funny to us in management is that when he's playing for the Royals, he's still a Raider.

"That is strange to us. But we're excited about him playing two professional sports. We really are. A lot of people don't think we are. But we are."

LoCasale paused.

"He might become the first Raider to win the American League Most Valuable Player award," he said. "Imagine that. How can we not be proud of that?"

□

The clock wound down. Fifty-seven seconds, 56, 55. . . .

Bo Jackson sauntered off the field at the Los Angeles Memorial Coliseum, his Raiders helmet hanging from the tips of his fingers, the sun setting in the distance.

His head tilted to one side, Bo cracked a smile. He was satisfied with his—and the team's—play on this the ninth Sunday of the 1989 NFL season.

Jackson's Raiders, after all, were putting the finishing touches on a convincing 28-7 triumph over the Cincinnati Bengals. And Bo already had put the finishing touches on a scintillating performance: 159 yards rushing

Bo, wearing a big smile, arrives for his first day of football duty after completing his 1989 baseball season with the Kansas City Royals.

(92 on one burst, of course) and two touchdowns.

As Bo headed toward the Raiders' bench, with all heads flashing toward the imposing figure wearing silver-and-black jersey No. 34, a familiar face approached the two-sport wonder. It was baseball star Eric Davis.

What was the Cincinnati Reds' slugger doing at the Los Angeles Coliseum? Visiting his friends among the Bengals?

"Partly," he replied, cracking a smile.

"You should know why I'm here," he said. "To see Bo. Probably everybody's here to see Bo."

And what did Davis think of Bo's performance?

"What can you say, the man is magnificent," Davis said. "To do what he's doing, well, it's phenomenal. Really. I can't imagine anyone doing this, playing two sports professionally.

". . . I really can't believe he's doing it, especially after the baseball season he just had. He put up MVP numbers. I thought he might kiss football goodbye. But here he is, taking this pounding.

"That's the thing that's really shocking me. The pounding he takes. All those hits. But obviously it doesn't affect him much. He's a better athlete than I ever thought he was."

□

Cincinnati defensive back Eric Thomas doesn't mince words when talking about Bo.

"Bo Jackson's the best running back in football, maybe the best running back of all time," Thomas said.

"I didn't think he was this good. Or should I say great."

Thomas had spent a better part of an autumn afternoon in 1989 with his neck turned as he watched Bo streak downfield.

"Baseball players shouldn't come in and do what he did to us," Thomas said. "It was like he hit three home runs against us.

"I can't imagine a baseball player doing this to us (bolting 92 yards on one play and rushing for 159 overall)—or anybody in the NFL, for that matter. What's really so remarkable is for him to come in here after the baseball season, take this kind of beating and not even flinch. Like it doesn't matter. Like it doesn't bother him.

"That's the feeling I got from him. He's like a superman. We have a great secondary here and he did a number on us. That 92-yard run was something else. He really turned it on. His speed was devastating. For a running back his size to run that fast, a definite 4.1, it just doesn't seem possible.

"I think he surprised everyone. He surprised me, that's for sure. On his touchdown run, the play was to the weakside. Nothing special. Backs

Tim McDonald of Phoenix discovers the hard way that tackling Bo Jackson is not an easy proposition.

usually gain four or five yards on that. I've never seen a back run it back the way he did.

"I came up to force him wide. But he dipped inside, went back outside and was gone. Outran everyone. He shocked every one of us on that play. Every one of us."

□

When Raiders quarterback Jay Schroeder was asked about the most memorable Bo Jackson play he had seen, he didn't choose one of the "storied" Bo feats. Forget about the 90 yards-plus touchdown jaunts and the run-ins with Mike Harden, Brian Bosworth and Rickey Dixon.

"On a play against Seattle (in 1988), Bo ran the ball up the middle," Schroeder recalled. "He ran into four, maybe five, Seahawks. I was hit and was on the ground.

"I figured the play was over. I got up and started walking toward the sidelines. Suddenly, I see Bo downfield. I said to myself, 'What's he doing down there?'

"The guy gained 14 yards on the play. Fourteen yards! I couldn't believe it. There was no way in the world anyone could have gotten a yard out of that play, the way those Seahawks piled up the middle.

"When Bo got back to the huddle, I said, 'How'd you do that?' Typically, he just shrugged. Said nothing.

"I made a mental note to myself that I'd review that play on film. I was so curious, so fascinated with this guy and how he made that play go."

After seeing the replay, Schroeder was even more startled.

"Bo runs straight up the middle," the quarterback explained, "smacks right into a wall of Seahawks, then suddenly goes underneath the pile. He went underneath!

"His legs are so strong and he has so much balance that he was able to get down low, push guys away with his strength and break away. He runs so low to the ground that you can't tackle him. You can't get a good piece of him. One guy bounced off his thigh.

"I had never seen anyone do that before—gain that much yardage on a play like that, the way Bo did. I don't think anyone could do that.

"Except Bo."

□

Quarterback Jay Schroeder had noticed the article in the newspaper in November 1987. He didn't believe it.

"I read where Bo had worked for only three days before his first game with the Raiders, then went out and gained 14 yards on his first play and

Jay Schroeder, who once played baseball in the Toronto Blue Jays organization before becoming a successful NFL quarterback, is amazed that Bo can compete successfully in both sports at the same time.

ran 10 times (eight, actually) for something like 40 yards (37)," said Schroeder, who was a member of the Washington Redskins at the time.

"That ain't bad for a Hall of Famer, let alone a guy who had just finished playing about 130 professional baseball games (Bo had appeared in 116 for the Kansas City Royals in '87) and worked out for three days before playing a professional football game. Think about that for a second. If that's not incredible, on an athletic scale, nothing is."

Still, Schroeder needed some real convincing. He got it in 1989.

"He played nearly the entire baseball season," Schroeder said, "won the MVP in the All-Star Game, put up MVP numbers for the season, comes in here, works out for three days, lifts some weights and bam! He goes out and runs for 85—85!—yards (against the Kansas City Chiefs, on 11 carries).

"I'm saying, 'Come on. This can't be for real. This is too much for a human being to do. The body and mind can't do this.' "

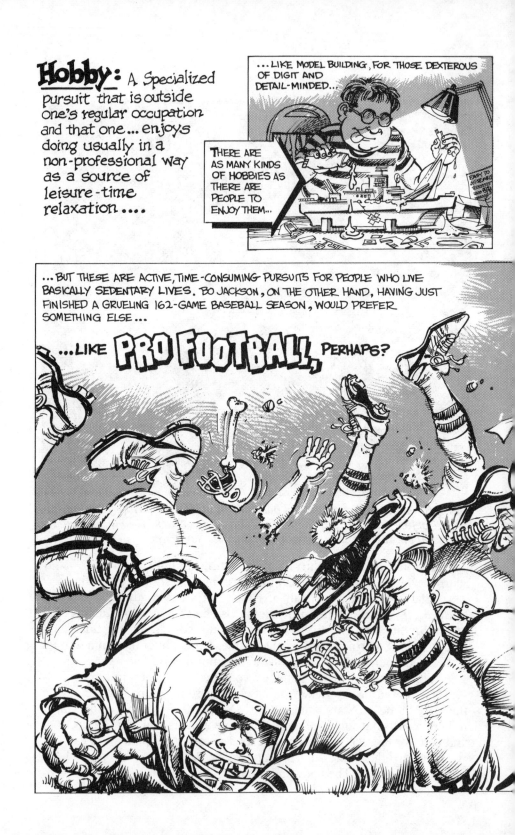

ONE OTHER BIG DIFFERENCE BETWEEN BO'S HOBBY AND EVERYONE ELSE'S — MOST PEOPLE'S HOBBIES DON'T CAUSE **CASUALTIES**!?

...WHICH IS WHAT MIKE HARDEN BECAME, IN BO'S FOURTH NFL GAME —

DID ANYBODY GET THE LICENSE NUMBER OF THAT TRUCK?

SURE, MIKE — SURE! IT WAS NUMBER 34!?

SPECTACULAR END ZONE RUNS WERE SOON BECOMING SO COMMONPLACE THAT RAIDERS COACH ART SHELL WAS GETTING A BIT SPOILED —

CAN'T BREAK 'EM ALL, COACH. GOTTA MIX IN A FEW 20-YARD GAINS EVERY NOW AND THEN!?

WHAT THE HELL'S GOING ON? YOU HAD THE CHANCE TO BREAK ANOTHER LONG ONE. WHAT HAPPENED?

THEN, AN INTERESTING STATEMENT BY SAFETY EDDIE ANDERSON GAVE BO NOTORIETY OF A DIFFERENT SORT:

He's like a wild turkey... Never could catch one easy — They're shifty creatures!

YET, **STILL** THERE WERE DOUBTING THOMASES — THOSE WHO FELT THAT BO HAD STILL NOT BEEN PUT TO A TRUE TEST — BUT THAT TEST WAS COMING...

NOW, EVERY FARM SOUTH OF CANADA HAS A TURKEY NICKNAMED "BO" — AND THE TURKEYS ARE NONE TOO HAPPY ABOUT IT!

Bo Knows. . .

Nike turned Bo Jackson into a commercial superstar with its "Bo Knows" commercial that was introduced during baseball's 1989 All-Star Game telecast. During filming for the commercial, Bo competed in such sports as cricket (above left), tennis (below left), soccer (above right) and hockey (above), with stars from the different events proclaiming that Bo also "knows" their specific sports, as well as his more familiar professional pursuits of baseball and football. Bo, of course, rose to the occasion on the night of the "Bo Knows" spot by winning the All-Star Game's MVP citation, proving that timing is everything in the marketing world.

A Tale of Two Seasons

Vincent Edward Jackson
(Bo)

Born November 30, 1962, at Bessemer, Ala.
Height, 6.01. Weight, 222.
Throws and bats righthanded.
Attended Auburn University, Auburn, Ala.

Baseball Record

Shares major league records for most strikeouts, nine-inning game (5), April 18, 1987; most strikeouts, inning (2), April 8, 1987, fourth inning.
Major League stolen bases: 1986 (3), 1987 (10), 1988 (27), 1989 (26). Total—66.
Led American League batters in strikeouts with 172 in 1989.

Year Club	League	Pos.	G.	AB.	R.	H.	2B.	3B.	HR.	RBI.	B.A.	PO.	A.	E.	F.A.
1986—Memphis†	South.	OF	53	184	30	51	9	3	7	25	.277	116	8	7	.947
1986—Kansas City	Amer.	OF	25	82	9	17	2	1	2	9	.207	29	2	4	.886
1987—Kansas City	Amer.	OF	116	396	46	93	17	2	22	53	.235	180	9	9	.955
1988—Kansas City‡	Amer.	OF	124	439	63	108	16	4	25	68	.246	246	11	7	.973
1989—Kansas City§	Amer.	OF	135	515	86	132	15	6	32	105	.256	224	11	8	.967
Major League Totals—4 Years			400	1432	204	350	50	13	81	235	.244	679	33	28	.962

Selected by New York Yankees' organization in 2nd round of free-agent draft, June 7, 1982.
Selected by California Angels' organization in 20th round of free-agent draft, June 3, 1985.
Selected by Kansas City Royals' organization in 4th round of free-agent draft, June 2, 1986.
†On temporary inactive list, June 20 to June 30, 1986.
‡On disabled list, June 1 to July 2, 1988.
§On disabled list, July 25 to August 9, 1989.

ALL-STAR GAME RECORD

Shares All-Star Game record for hitting home run in first at-bat, July 11, 1989.

Year League	Pos.	AB.	R.	H.	2B.	3B.	HR.	RBI.	B.A.	PO.	A.	E.	F.A.
1989—American	OF	4	1	2	0	0	1	2	.500	2	0	0	1.000

Football Record

Heisman Trophy winner, 1985.
Named college football Player of the Year by THE SPORTING NEWS, 1985.
Named as running back on THE SPORTING NEWS College All-America Team, 1985.
Selected by Tampa Bay in 1st round (1st player selected) of 1986 NFL draft.
Selected by Birmingham in 1986 USFL territorial draft.
On reserve/did not sign entire 1986 football season through April 27, 1987.
Selected by Los Angeles Raiders in 7th round (183rd player selected) of 1987 NFL draft.
Signed by Los Angeles Raiders, July 17, 1987.
On reserve/did not report, August 27 through October 23, 1987; activated, October 24, 1987.
On reserve/did not report, August 22 through October 11, 1988; reported, October 12, 1988.
Activated from reserve/did not report, October 15, 1988.
On reserve/did not report, July 21 through October 10, 1989; activated, October 11, 1989.

Year Club		——RUSHING——				PASS RECEIVING				—TOTAL—		
	G.	Att.	Yds.	Avg.	TD.	P.C.	Yds.	Avg.	TD.	TD.	Pts.	F.
1987—Los Angeles Raiders NFL	7	81	554	6.8	4	16	136	8.5	2	6	36	2
1988—Los Angeles Raiders NFL	10	136	580	4.3	3	9	79	8.8	0	3	18	5
1989—Los Angeles Raiders NFL	11	173	950	5.5	4	9	69	7.7	0	4	24	1
Pro Totals—3 Years	28	390	2084	5.3	11	34	284	8.4	2	13	78	8

Additional pro statistics: Recovered one fumble, 1987; recovered two fumbles, 1988.